GW00599683

TWINS

TWINS

Carola Zentner

DAVID & CHARLES
Newton Abbot   London
North Pomfret (VT)   Vancouver

ISBN 0 7153 6997 0

Library of Congress Catalog Card Number 75-2914

Set in 11 on 13pt Linotype Baskerville and printed in
Great Britain by Latimer Trend & Company Ltd Plymouth
for David & Charles (Holdings) Limited
South Devon House   Newton Abbot   Devon

Published in the United States of America
by David & Charles Inc
North Pomfret   Vermont 05053   USA

Published in Canada
by Douglas David & Charles Limited
132 Philip Avenue   North Vancouver   BC

Contents

Preface

My qualifications for writing this book are called Adam and Laurence, Marcus and Quentin. They came in two sets, twenty-one months apart and are fraternal. Individually and together they posed practical problems which had to be solved by trial and error. Whereas most people have friends and relations who can be counted on to give (good and bad) advice on bringing up a baby, the birth of twins can be completely outside their experience. What mothers need at such a time is reassurance. Reassurance from people who know what it is all about, who have had twins themselves and who know the answers to some of the questions which may arise.

Most books about twins, and there aren't very many, are learned and scientific tomes, written for learned and scientific people. This is a practical book written for parents and based on the experience of parents. It is written in the hope that others will derive as much joy from their twins as I have. Since I am neither a doctor, nor a geneticist nor a psychologist, facts and figures which I have considered to be of interest, come—with my grateful thanks—from Dr A. J. Costello, of the Medical Research Council Environmental Factors Unit, and others qualified to talk or write about them.

To all parents of little girls, I would hasten to point out that no sexist slant is intended by the use of 'he' throughout the text; but the repetition of 'he or she' would be both cumbersome and boring.

For the rest, I thank most warmly all the twins and triplets and their parents for sharing their experiences with me. And I have to thank my own twins for occasionally allowing me to write this book instead of playing Monopoly with them. C. Z.

Introduction

In the Western world today, the arrival of twins provokes only great interest and delight. The arrival of identical twins, with the attendant problems of identification and the potential for hilarious confusion, merely adds to this general merriment. This has not always been the case; in primitive societies, and in myth and legend, twins were frequently eyed with fear and suspicion. They were thought to have supernatural powers and were frequently cast out of society as evil beings. Their conception was taken to be unnatural, either the result of adultery or the intervention of a deity. The worst thing one could wish a women in West Africa, according to Amram Scheinfeld in *Twins and Supertwins*, was 'May you become the mother of twins!' It may be that such fears had their origin in the difficulties of feeding and looking after extra babies when a tribe wandered and struggled for survival.

In most of Africa, north-east Asia and parts of India, the fate of mother and twins was miserable to say the least. The *Encyclopaedia of Religion and Ethics* (1921) remarks that 'twin births provoked terror, fear, repugnance, suspicion, anxiety, perplexity, hope and joy'. Hope and joy were certainly limited since the twins were often thought to have committed a crime which would call down the vengeance of the highers powers. Death was the penalty. Even where the birth was interpreted as a message from heaven, it was still taken to be one of evil about to befall the tribe; again, the twins forfeited their lives, although occasionally they were subjected to superstitious practices designed to avert catastrophe.

In ancient times, such beliefs were reported among the Assyrians, Babylonians and Egyptians. As recently as 1905,

11

mothers of twins in the Niger Delta were still being condemned to spend the rest of their lives as outcasts in the forests. Among the Ibos, twin births defiled the whole quarter and the inhabitants were forced to throw away all half-burnt firewood and any food cooked or water brought in during the previous night. In Zululand, twins were not counted at all in the number of children in a family. In Uganda, although they were thought to be scarcely human, twins were nevertheless credited with being wild and fearless, and were especially sought out to lead the attacking army in war. In the Benin region of Nigeria, mothers of twins were sent away, but a rich husband could keep his wife, provided another victim took her place and spent twelve months in the 'twin town' so as to be cleansed.

The life and times of twins among the American Indians was often considerably better. Some tribes dressed them in magnificent clothes; others thought the birth of twins a great honour for the mother. The Mohave treated twins with great impartiality, believing that if one was given more than his share the other would get angry and return to the place from which he came, and that if one died the other would die too. Among the Cocopas, twins were thought to come from heaven and only paying a visit to earth. They were held in special regard and treated with affection, since it was assumed that, if they did not like it here, they would return to heaven. In another tribe, the second twin was not considered a real person at all and was killed.

The paternity of twins was not always credited where it belonged. The Salivas on the Orinoco in South America thought that the mother had committed adultery, and assuming that the second twin had a different father from the first, whipped the mother as a punishment. Medically speaking, it is possible, although exceedingly rare, for fraternal twins to have different fathers, but a few cases are recorded where blood tests have established a different father for each twin. The Shuswap Indians believed a twin birth had been influenced by a grizzly bear or a deer, or was caused by eating double fruit, particularly nuts.

Fear of incest was uppermost in the minds of some primitive people. The Yurok Indians suffocated the female of a male/female pair believing that incest would otherwise take place. In parts of India, nine months' intimacy in the womb was considered sinful. In Bali, however, where no proscribed marriage relationships existed, boy/girl twins were considered 'betrothed' and forced to marry.

In regions where twins had a favourable status, much ritual attended their birth. In one region of West Africa, it was celebrated by a feast of eggs and beans, boiled with the leaves of a special shrub, which was eaten by all past and present mothers of twins. In Lomeland, an old woman, herself the mother of twins, led the father and mother round the house in opposite directions and in again, so that the newborn twins would not die. Four months later, the twins were taken out, preceded by two flute players playing the 'twin march'. They visited a place where women who had previously had twins offered goods for sale. The old woman made a symbolic purchase for the new twins, who would then 'have been to market'. Only then was the mother allowed to leave the house for the first time.

A different ceremonial attended Egyptian twins, who were thought capable of changing shape and turning into cats at night, in order to steal milk, food and chickens. This could be prevented, it seems, if the father put them in a cold oven immediately after birth!

The naming of twins was not always a matter of the parents' choice. Among the Bantu, all the boys were given the same names—Aburi and Nobese—and the girls were called Abuda and Tandabo, which must have led to a great deal of confusion in families with more than one set. The Balubas gave all boy twins the names of former twin kings, Kyungu and Kahya, who were thought to have gone mad.

South American Indians, who recognised that a special affinity existed between twins, carved little likenesses of them and, if one died, its effigy was given to the survivor to protect him from loneliness. The African Yorubas, too, carved special twin figures which were kept in family shrines; if one baby died, the figure continued to be washed and dressed like the living twin.

In legend, the birth of twins takes strange forms. The Kiowa Indians have a legend that speaks of twins as split or half boys, the result of a boy playing with a hoop. He is forbidden to throw it upwards, but he does so and it hits him on the head when it comes down. When he looks round, he finds a replica of himself. Among the Micmac and Passamaquaddy Indians, the younger twin, called 'Wolf', was thought to have started life rather violently by bursting through his mother's side, thereby killing her.

In Western mythology, the best-known twins are un-doubtedly Castor and Pollux, known as the Dioscuri. They and their sister Helen were the children of Leda and, in one version of their birth, they emerged from an egg. Although Tyndareus, king of Sparta, who was Leda's husband, was regarded by Homer as their father, others credit him only with Castor's paternity, Pollux and Helen being fathered by Zeus, king of the gods. As a result, Castor was mortal as he had a mortal father, while Pollux was immortal. However, Pollux shared his immortality with his twin brother by alternately spending a day on earth with him and a day with the gods. Their permanent memorial is the heavenly constellation known as Gemini or The Twins.

Other twins to be found in Greek and Latin mythology are Apollo and Diana, the winds Calais and Zetes, and Aedulus and Beotus, the twin sons of Neptune.

In legend, Romulus and Remus, twin sons of the vestal virgins, who were suckled by a wolf, were the founders of Rome, and also of Siena which has a wolf and the twins as its emblem. The two came to a sticky end as Romulus killed his brother and then disappeared in a symbolic thunderstorm.

Even those unfamiliar with the Bible will know that it contains one set of twins, Jacob and Esau, who were obviously fraternal since Jacob says: 'Behold, Esau my brother is a hairy man, and I am a smooth man.' (Genesis 27:11.) Followers of the Vedic faith in India worshipped the twin gods Asvin, who symbolised all things good. Apart from being inseparable, they were beautiful, strong, clever, compassionate and capable of working miracles. They could make the old young, cripples walk, and the wives of the impotent bear children. With such gifts to distribute, it is not surprising that the Rig-Veda contains fifty hymns dedicated to Asvin and that these were chanted three times a day in sacrificial rites.

Twins play their part in literature too. Those who write about them are often twins themselves or the fathers of twins. Shakespeare, reputed to be the father of twins Hamnet and Judith, created great confusion in his *Comedy of Errors* with two sets of identical twins, and the plot in *Twelfth Night* revolves around a mix-up over Viola and her twin brother Sebastian.

Thornton Wilder, himself a twin, used twins in *The Bridge of San Luis Rey*, while Mark Twain, who sometimes pretended to be a twin, wrote about twin situations on several occasions. In Hal Holbrook's *Mark Twain Tonight* he is quoted as telling a reporter: 'My twin and I got mixed up in the bathtub when we were only two weeks old and one of us drowned but we didn't know which. Some think it was Bill and some think it was me. One of us had a peculiar mark—a large mole on the back of his left hand; that was me. That child was the one that was drowned!'

Other writers who explored the intricacies of twin relationships included Georges Sand, Alexandre Dumas and the Brothers Grimm.

When one turns to the past, although some twins must

have made their mark, they were not remembered as such. Perhaps that is why an unknown biologist wrote in 1869, 'No one has ever become famous who had a twin brother.' However, the French royal house of Bourbon had several sets of twins; Louis XV was himself the father of twin girls. Knowing the royal wish for an heir presumptive, the obstetrician on delivering them was heard to say, 'Cela ne vaut pas un dauphin.' They were subsequently known as Madame Première and Madame Seconde.* There were also plenty of twins in the German royal houses of Hesse, Baden, and Bavaria and in the Austrian Habsburg dynasty.

There is one present-day twin ruler—the Shah of Persia. His sister, the Princess Ashraf, who is a dedicated human rights worker, was born first, but the law of succession gave him the Peacock Throne. King Hussein of Jordan is the father of twins, but they are not his first children.

Famous personalities who are parents of twins include Mia Farrow and André Previn, Ingrid Bergman, Mohammed Ali and Alan Bates. Twins who became celebrated in their own right have been the Dolly Sisters, the film-making Boulting brothers, the cricket-playing Bedsers and the French undersea explorers, Jean and Auguste Picard. Two identical brothers, Richard and David Atcherley, both reached the rank of air vice marshal while serving in the Royal Air Force. Another pair of identical twins, Ross and Norris McWhirter, are joint editors of *The Guinness Book of Records*, which is something of a record in itself. Last and certainly least, the Kray twins earned themselves widespread notoriety for their underworld activities which have put them behind bars for a long time to come.

*Cabanès. *Moeurs intimes du Passé* (Paris 1923)

1 What Makes for Twins

One of us was born a twin
Yet not a soul knew which

H. S. Leigh in 'THE TWINS'

The first question asked by friends and acquaintances when they discover you are going to have twins is whether there are any twins in your family or in your husband's. Once they are born, everybody—including yourself—wants to know what sex they are and if they are identical or fraternal. Many people still assume that twins must resemble one another and few have any idea of the frequency of twinning.

Starting at square one, twins are conceived either as one egg, which splits into two within a few days of conception, or as two eggs, which have been fertilised by separate male sperms. One-egg (monozygotic) twins are identical and of the same sex; two-egg (dizygotic) twins are fraternal. Triplets, quads or more, can come from one egg which has divided, or from one egg each or from a mixture of the two.

It is accepted that these are the only kinds of twins, although in 1916 a theory was put forward by C. H. Danforth that there might be a third type. Certain twins appeared to have characteristics stemming from their mother but not apparent on the father's side, and Danforth suggested that this could be the result of the fertilisation of two eggs which had not been released independently. The theory was not confirmed by subsequent evidence, however, and it is better not to complicate the issue with hypotheses.

The sex of a baby is determined by the male but, as this is not a conscious determination, we have to wait until it is born before we know if it is a boy or a girl. Medical research may soon correct this situation, but meanwhile, for parents who have set their hearts on one sex rather than the other, twins at least provide a double chance of getting what they want.

The figures for two recent years in England and Wales show that a marginally higher proportion of twins are of the same sex, boys slightly outnumbering girls:

Twins	1970	1971
2 male	2,705	2,619
2 female	2,468	2,585
1 of each	2,393	2,389

At birth, the sex of the twins is quickly determined, although one husband's charming but uninformative reply to his wife's question, 'What is it?', after the first twin emerged, was 'It's beautiful!' It is not always so simple to establish whether twins are identical or fraternal. If one is a boy and the other a girl, they are clearly fraternal, since identical twins are always of the same sex. Fraternal twins, too, will normally have separate membranes round them and a placenta each, although these placentae may have fused. To discover the zygosity, or twin relationship, of twins of the same sex, it is possible in many cases for the naked and inexperienced eye to determine without any doubt that they are identical simply by comparing their physical features. Have a good look at the twins when placed side by side. Examine the colour and shape of their eyes, the colour of the hair and which way the whorl goes, the shape of the nose and mouth. Compare them feature by feature and, if they are the same, then the twins are identical, even though they may be of different weight and height. If there are distinct physical differences, then the twins are almost certainly fraternal.

The exception to this guide line could occur when two identical twins are born with very disparate weights. Should one, for instance, weigh 6lb at birth and the other $3\frac{1}{2}$lb, the degree of their development could be sufficiently different for them to look quite unalike. In such cases, it can take up to two years before these differences fade.

If there is any doubt and it is important to know for certain, a blood test will establish whether the twins belong to the same blood group or not; however, since babies are not pincushions, nobody will want to stick needles into them unnecessarily. The other completely conclusive test is through a skin graft. Except in cases of medical need, when it could be a life saver, this would not be carried out from pure curiosity. Human beings reject skin tissue other than their own, with the exception of identical twins who will accept each other's. Equally, transplants will take from one twin to another.

Examination of the membranes around the babies can provide evidence of their twin relationship, but this is a time-consuming procedure and not always conclusive. Each foetus is surrounded by two membranes: the inner one called the amnion and the outer called the chorion. If the division of identical twins occurs in the first week of pregnancy, each will have two separate membranes and will therefore appear the same as fraternal twins. If the inner cell mass separates a few days later, the twins will share a chorion, but still have separate amnia. If they separate a few days later still, each will have one chorion and one amnion. The latter will always be identical but, since by no means all identical twins are cocooned together in this way, it is of more interest to scientists than to parents how many separate or shared membranes their babies had.

It used to be a popular belief that identical twins shared a placenta, but that fraternals had one each. In fact, it is not so simple as that. Two-thirds of identical twins share a placenta, while the other third and all fraternals start off with one each. But if, after floating around for the first week of pregnancy, the ones with a separate placenta become implanted close together in the tissue of the uterus, the placentae may fuse. This makes it difficult to establish their relationship, since the frequency of fused placentae is the same for both types.

Nor is there any evidence to support the theory that one identical twin is the mirror image of the other—that one will be right handed and the other left handed or that one will have certain organs on the opposite side to his twin. Any of these factors is as rare (or common) in twins as it is in other children.

The chances of having identical twins are much smaller than of having fraternals. Figures show that only between a quarter and a third of twins born are identical, or between $3\frac{1}{2}$ and 4 per 1,000 births.

Weinberg's method, the rule of thumb for estimating the relative numbers of identical and fraternal twins, is based on the expectation that there will be as many twins of the same sex as of the opposite sex among fraternal twins, whereas identical twins will all be in pairs of the same sex. If, therefore, the number of unlike sex pairs is subtracted from the number of like sex pairs, the difference represents approximately the number of identical pairs, while the number of fraternal pairs is twice the number of unlike sex pairs. However, this is only approximate because the number of male births is slightly greater than female births.

There are virtually no variations in the frequency of identical-twin births in the Western world, but in Japan and the Far East the incidence is slightly higher. It is thought that the apparently greater proportion of identicals has been wrongly interpreted because the fraternal twinning rate there is very low and because hospitals—whose records provide the statistics—will give preferential admission to the mother having a first baby and she will have a much smaller chance of giving birth to fraternal twins.

Heredity and maternal age have a great bearing on the production of fraternal twins, but this is not the case with identicals, who are almost as likely to be born to the mother in her early twenties with no previous pregnancies as to the older mother who runs a marginally higher risk. Although Hippocrates, the grandfather of medicine, believed that twins were conceived as a result of sperm splitting into two, and others have thought that particularly 'aggressive' sperm were capable of splitting the female egg, hereditary factors are largely discounted in the production of identical twins.

When it comes to fraternal twins, much more is known about the why and wherefore. To begin with, credit or blame for double ovulation, which leads to fraternal twins, can only be laid at the door of the female. Although the fraternal-twin tendency can be handed down through the male, it can only manifest itself in the female's physiological make up. A husband who is a twin, therefore, has no hereditary influence on the pregnancies of his wife. His daughters, however, will carry the recessive genes which may, in turn, make them mothers of fraternal twins.

So the mother of twins can inherit the tendency from either parent but, even if her husband has a family tree liberally laden with twins, she will not produce twins because of his inheritance. His daughters and granddaughters, however, will carry the genes which will then increase their chances of giving birth to twins.

Four main factors govern the production of fraternal twins: race, maternal age, number of previous births and heredity.

The highest fraternal twinning rate exists among African negroes with a ratio of 16: 1,000 births. Whites, including Indians, have half that number, that is 8: 1,000, and Asiatics a low rate of 4: 1,000. Forgetting about the incidence of identical twins, which is almost constant at between 3 and 4 per 1,000, the fraternal rate per 1,000 varies from 5·9 in Spain to 7·1 in France, 8·1 in Holland, and 8·9 in England and Wales. Since these figures were compiled in 1960, the odds have lengthened slightly, but it still means that, theoretically anyway, every forty-ninth person walking down the street or catching the 9.15 is a twin.

Where races have become mixed, the fraternal twinning rate finds a level between the two component races. This is why, in North America, for example, the negro race which has over the years intermarried with other races, has a lower rate than African negroes but a higher rate than North American whites.

The likelihood of having fraternal twins increases sharply with age. The graph starts from a low point at 20 and rises in a steady uphill curve so that at 35 the risk is three times as great as at 20. The risk remains at the same level until the age of 40 when it drops again. The probability also increases with successive pregnancies, the fifth being the biggest twin-producer.

Why older women are more likely to have twins is not known, but it is generally thought to be due to a less well-functioning reproductive system. Or perhaps the stepping up of egg production is just a question of nature ensuring an adequate replenishment of the species before the shutters come down!

However, as effective contraception becomes more widely practised throughout the world and as women in the West marry younger and finish having a family at a lower age, the number of twins born may decrease. In Ireland, for example, where girls marry well into their twenties and where birth control is not practised, the twinning rate was 1 in 67 births, but in England and Wales it has been dropping since its post-war boom. From 12.59 twin births per 1,000 in 1951–6, the rate had dropped to 11.38 per 1,000—a ratio of 1 to 87 maternities —by 1962; to 1:94 by 1968 and to 1:96 by 1970. The total birth rate for England and Wales in 1970 was 784,486 with 15,499 twin births. In 1971, although the birth rate fell to 783,155, the number of live twins born remained the same at 15,499. The number of twin maternities for 1970 was 8,042, showing a ratio of 97:55; in 1971 there were 8,000 maternities, so the ratio was 97:89. It remains to be seen whether the rate continues to fall.

Although there is a national average figure concerning the incidence of twins, there is no doubt that certain women are more likely to become twin mothers than others. In fact, it is thought that, since fraternal twinning is controlled by a completely recessive gene, in Caucasians (whites) this is present in about a quarter of population who have a twinning rate of about 32 : 1,000 (Bulmer). So mothers of twins present or future are not a random selection of women but a marked minority.

In this minority are close relatives of mothers of twins whose risk is sharply increased. Sisters of twin mothers have $2\frac{1}{2}$ times the general rate and sisters of fraternal twins have 4 times the rate. In the case of grandmothers still of child-bearing age, whose daughters have given birth to fraternal twins, they themselves run twice the risk of the general population according to Weinberg.

Apart from the propensity of certain categories of women to have twins for reasons of age and inheritance, there are three other noteworthy factors. First, there is a slightly higher twinning rate among women who conceive in the first three months of marriage. This may be due to more frequent intercourse, allowing a second ovum to be fertilised a little while after the first. Second, there appears to be a correlation between twinning rates and nutrition. It is known that, among mammals, undernutrition results in smaller litters. The practice of 'flushing' sheep—that is, to feed them up before mating—is widespread because it leads to a larger number of lambs. Among wild animals, litter sizes are also bigger in years when food is plentiful. On the human level, although nobody has tried to feed women up in order to make them have twins, tables compiled by M. G. Bulmer of the incidence of dizygotic twinning in European countries during the war years of 1941–5 show a slight drop where food was scarce, compared with those countries where adequate supplies were maintained.

The third, small but significant, category of women much more likely to have multiple births are those who have been treated with fertility drugs. A certain percentage of women, unable to conceive because they fail to ovulate, may be treated with either Clomiphene or Gonadotrophin. Clomiphene is a chemical compound which stimulates the release of natural gonadotrophin from the pituitary gland. Gonadotrophin stimulates the ovaries to produce eggs and, because its effect cannot be controlled as it is when it occurs naturally, there is an increased likelihood of twinning. A woman treated with Clomiphene, also known as Clomid, has a one-in-forty chance of having more than one baby. With Gonadotrophin, the risk is one in four. Any twins born as a result of treatment with fertility drugs will be fraternal although, in theory at least, any one of the artificially stimulated female eggs could split after conception, resulting in identical twins. Certainly, any woman offered fertility drugs should be aware of the possible consequences.

For some reason, it is generally assumed to be very unlikely that a woman will produce a second set of twins. Nothing is farther from the truth, and it is as well to be forewarned before you embark on increasing your family, lest the increases always come in twos. Whereas the average combined twinning rate for fraternals and identicals is between 9 and 12 per 1,000 births, the statistics taken from a Manchester sample show a rise to 47 per 1,000 for a repeat performance. For mothers of fraternal triplets, the risk of producing twins in a subsequent pregnancy rises to nine times that of the general population, and those with quads run sixteen times the risk.

In practice, it appears that parents of twins tend to feel that their family is complete and do not intend increasing its size. However, this information comes from a contemporary longitudinal study of twins and their families and, as the eldest twins are at present only three years old, it is too early to say whether the parents might change their minds. And, of course, not every baby is planned, so that twin-prone mothers may find themselves with little accidents that are in the plural.

2 The Prospect of Twins

All who joy would win
Must share it—
Happiness was born a twin

Byron

Few mothers-to-be react to the prospect of twins with complete equanimity, indeed, most react quite violently. They may be utterly thrilled, and panting to tell every friend, relation and passer-by the good news, or become a trembling bag of nerves, in need of moral support. After a few hours, as with most unexpected news, it becomes part and parcel of life, to be lived with and accepted as a fact. Both mental and physical adjustments are needed; if preparations have been made for one, quite a number of practical arrangements will be necessary to ensure that everything is ready for a second baby as well.

If the twins are the first children, then you will get your baptism of fire in a concentrated dose, because you will not have much of an idea what makes one baby tick, let alone two. But you can rest assured that you will learn to cope and can comfort yourself with the knowledge that any subsequent (single) children you may have will be as easy as pie to look after. Even if, like some, you go on to have another set of twins, apart from becoming a veritable curiosity to be pointed out in the street, the problems presented will also resolve themselves.

Before there is any need to get to grips with the reality of twins, take time off to wonder at the marvel of producing two babies at the same time. To begin with, you are kaleidoscoping eighteen months into nine: two babies for the price of one pregnancy; nine months of normal girth, energy and well being; one labour instead of two; one concentrated period—instead of consecutive ones—of involvement with baby problems, dirty nappies, preparing bottles, getting up for feeds when you don't feel like it.

Then there is the enormous admiration which the twins will arouse in other maternal (and paternal) breasts. One pram, one baby, is a common enough sight. Two babies in one pram are fascinating for all and, if you are short of friends or have just moved to a new locality, never fear that yours will be the fate of the lonely mother. Every outing into the park or to the shops will be punctuated by conversations with people whose ages will range from five to eighty, wanting detailed information about your twins. Everyone will assume that they are identical, even if they are not, most people being more or less incapable of telling two identically aged boys or girls apart, mainly because they do not look very carefully. As for you, you will be able to tell them apart soon enough. It's a question of concentrated exposure, studying them in detail to find the differences which, with identicals, may not be perceptible to the casual onlooker but are quite conclusive to the parents. As time goes on, the differences will, in any case, become more apparent to parents and not less so. With fraternals, there is no difficulty anyway.

Although comparison between the two should be strenuously avoided, nobody would deny parents the right to derive enormous interest, entertainment and pleasure from watching their twins grow up, of observing what remains a miracle, that you have two. Two asleep in their cots, frequently in the same position; two opening their mouths for a spoonful of lunch, like two little birds; two learning to crawl; two communicating with each other intelligibly before anyone else really understands their language. They have each other to play with while so many children are bored because they are on their own. And there is the advantage that twins have each other as allies to brave new circumstances together, like playgroup or school. Of course, there will also be two to gang up against you from time to time.

The practicalities of bringing up twins need not be of any immediate concern until after they are born. For the first ten days or so, they will anyway be looked after predominantly by doctors and nurses. Once they are home from hospital, what then? Newborn babies have pretty basic needs: feeds, baths and nappy changes are really only interruptions in their enormous capacity for sleep. So the introduction to twin motherhood should be reasonably gentle and it does not all happen at once. When my four boys were all under two, friends used to shake their heads in disbelief and ask over and over again, 'How do you cope?' The answer is that you learn to cope because problems arrive singly and intermittently. Little by little, you become more knowledgeable. You take one step at a time and the steps are quite small ones.

Much depends on the babies' temperament. A placid, contented baby is easy to keep that way, while a crotchety, restless one can pose more of a problem. The question is, which exists first—a fractious baby or a nervous mother? Are children born easy or difficult or do they become that way? Are good mothers born or are they made so by their children?

An experiment carried out in a London hospital throws a little light on the subject. Recordings were made of the heartbeats of two mothers. One tape recorded the regular heartbeats of a relaxed, calm woman; the other the quicker, jumpy heartbeats of a nervous and agitated woman. These recordings were amplified and played over a loudspeaker to the newborn infants in the hospital's nursery. The infants reacted very definitely: when the calm, regular heartbeats were played, they all slept peacefully; when the nervous ones were substituted, they all woke up and began to cry.

There are many factors, both physical and environmental, which effect a baby's temperament, and when both father and mother are hyper-active, lively people it is not surprising if their baby does not sleep all day. However, it does seem worth while making a conscious effort (if it does not come naturally) to be relaxed and calm with the babies because it will pay off big dividends. If you are relaxed in their company, you are all more likely to thrive. If not, you may be in for a tougher time than is necessary.

One mother found that her twins always acted up when she was trying to bundle them off quickly in order to get on with her accumulating housework. It was pointed out to her that her own attitude was probably responsible and that, if she put the chores out of her mind while she was with her children and concentrated on them, their demands might decrease; she found this to be absolutely true and learned a valuable lesson.

When that miracle of knowledge and efficiency, Isabella Beeton, wrote her book of household management, she devoted quite a few pages to the role and duties of the nursery governess, the upper nursemaid, under nursemaid, the monthly nurse, the wet nurse and the single nursemaid who might cope alone with just one housemaid in small families. The recommendations for the hiring and firing of nursery staff will today be more of entertainment value than practical interest. Nor will many mothers give more than a hollow laugh at Mrs Beeton's statement that 'an hour spent with the children will not be an hour wasted, even if it be one hard to spare'!

Although my book is written to help mothers cope single-handed with the reality of having twins, it is a wise principle never to turn down any offer of assistance unless it actually drives you up the wall. If a friend drops in for a chat at feeding time, hand her a baby and a bottle. If someone is around at bathtime, let her look after one while you do the other. If willing friends offer to shop for you, accept.

The most readily available help comes undoubtedly from a willing husband. Anyone married to the type of man who declares he does not know one end of a baby from the other should put a naked infant on his lap and let him find out! With luck though, he will belong to the modern school of husbands who treat their wives as equals and not as household slaves. With only one baby, a husband may prefer to opt out, but with two it is more difficult. As one husband put it: 'I could close my ears against the nocturnal wailing of our first baby quite easily. But when the twins were born I really didn't feel it would be fair to play the part of the hard-working breadwinner whose rest must not be disturbed. So we now take it in turns to get up.'

If it is a matter of importance for you to have your husband present at the birth, and if he wants to be there, it would be a good idea to make enquiries in the early stages of pregnancy about hospital procedure in this respect. Then, if one hospital's response is negative, there might be time to find another one with more enlightened ideas. Most couples who are together during the birth of their babies find that it adds immeasurably to the experience. Progressive hospitals recognise that the support given by the husband to his wife in labour may be invaluable, but some do not allow husbands to be present. In America recognition of the father's role during childbirth is even less common and some hospital boards have claimed that the father's presence 'would be unhealthy' and could lead to malpractice! Fortunately this sort of attitude is losing ground as public opinion changes.

In one London hospital, where it has been standard practice for years to encourage the father's participation at the birth, a cautionary tale used to be told to illustrate that not all men are suitable candidates. As the mother gave birth, the father fainted, fell down and broke his leg. The result was that he was in hospital for rather longer than his wife and child.

The first few years of motherhood leave little time for other things, but there is always an opportunity, however limited, to pursue some activity or pastime which will prevent frustration and perhaps boredom. If motherhood and domesticity are ends in themselves, there are unlikely to be any mental conflicts regarding the new way of life. If, however, life in the past has meant following a career, studying or having a hobby, do not make the mistake of assuming that all outside activities must come to an end. All work and no play makes Jill a very dull girl and a very frustrated mother as well.

Of course, you will have your hands full with a family to look after. If you have made a quick transition from bachelor girl in a bedsitter to wife and mother of two, living in a flat or house which is yours to care for, there will be plenty to do. Nevertheless, everybody—whether running the country or a home, with one child or ten—has only twenty-four hours in the day in which to do what is necessary. Everyone has to use some of those hours to get enough sleep; for the mother of young children this is particularly important, since nobody functions well or happily if she is exhausted. With Parkinson's admirable law which postulates that most jobs stretch or contract to fill the amount of time available, it is quite common to find the mother of one baby spending just as much time looking after it as another mother takes looking after several. Banish the thought that the good life is over and that a hard slog is all the future holds. It is up to you to retain your freedom and to continue getting out of life what you want. It is nearly always possible to find somebody to sit with the twins for a couple of hours, while you go to a class, or the cinema, or have your hair done.

It should not be assumed either that because there are babies around, social life for their parents comes to an end. Those who get into the habit of sitting stupefied in front of the television set night after night and moan about the difficulty of getting baby sitters just haven't tried. Unless you are in an isolated country area or if no one can be hired with confidence, where there are a number of young families living in close proximity, somebody is sure to have got a baby-sitting rota going. If there really isn't one, start it yourself. It does not strain the budget, because it costs nothing.

Friends invited to dinner or coffee are quite capable of understanding that there may not have been time to prepare a five-course *Cordon Bleu* meal. An hour or two spent with people you like, listening to stimulating conversation, is time well spent.

Don't become a bore in company though; resolve not to talk about the twins unless begged to do so. The fact that your kids are the brightest, most beautiful and charming children on earth, whose daily exploits are riveting and fascinating, is an incontrovertible fact. However, since your friends are either childless or also have the most beautiful, intelligent and advanced children, it is better to have a mutual non-aggression pact.

Apart from being enjoyable, doing what you want to do, away from the kids, even if only for an hour a week is, strangely enough, much more likely to help you to function well the rest of the time. Of the many mothers of twins whose experiences have gone into the writing of this book, those who have kept a sense of proportion about their double blessing have led much fuller and more satisfied lives than those who have assumed from the start that they would have no time to be anything other than mothers, wives and housewives. They have been happier and have also managed to transmit to their children the knowledge that mothers have some rights as well.

The prospect of twins may also bring financial worries with it. Obviously money does play a role and a sudden increase in outgoings resulting from the arrival of twins is not automatically followed by higher income. On the contrary, most breadwinners are only half way up the salary scale when commitments are at their heaviest, often with a newly acquired mortgage to be repaid, furniture to be bought and extra mouths to feed.

By means of judicious shopping, the generosity of grand-parents, and mutual aid schemes that mothers often set up, passing outgrown clothes, toys and equipment to each other, the extra expenses should not be a stumbling block. Bulk buying usually leads to discounts, and small advertisements and jumble sales can turn up marvellous bargains, leaving money to be spent on such labour-saving equipment as a good washing machine, which is a better investment than a carpet in the nursery.

Can the extra expense be met commercially? If the twins are bonny and particularly if they are identical, sooner or later someone will ask, 'Why don't you let them model, do commercials, endorse products?'

Although parents react differently to such a suggestion, it is fair comment that commercial exploitation will not benefit the children and may well harm them. A straight endorsement of a product might, in theory, produce extra cash for a minimal amount of public exposure; in practice, not only do few firms seek such tie-ups but they can go very sour. Many parents would not be happy at the thought of exposing their children to the artificial atmosphere created in such circumstances. Nor are the financial gains likely to offer sufficient inducement, such as an education paid for or a trust fund, to make it in any way worthwhile.

Another reason for not exploiting the situation is that most identical twins do not welcome the stares and attention they receive because of their similarity. They do not enjoy the curiosity of strangers, once they are old enough to be aware of it, and dislike the confusion they create in other people's eyes. With the exception of an occasional pair who take a theatrical delight in the effect they produce, most twins want to be seen as individuals. If fame comes their way, they want it for merit and not because of an accident of birth. Twins are not, therefore, likely to enjoy, and may well suffer if they are exposed to situations which accentuate their relationship.

When the children have grown up, that is a different matter because they can decide for themselves whether the financial rewards justify the publicity. In a home-perm advertising campaign of the 1950s, the slogan 'Which Twin has the Toni?' became a familiar catch phrase. More recently two middle-aged twins, both professional men, answered an advertisement seeking balding twins. Over quite a lengthy period, one twin had regular scalp treatments designed to promote the sponsor's baldness cure, while the other's hair, or lack of it, was left untouched. Every few months, together with a number of other middle-aged identical twins, they were flown to various exotic parts of the world, staying in luxury hotels with all expenses paid, to ensure suitable publicity for the opening of yet another scalp clinic. At the end of it all, the brothers were bald to the identical extent, the treatment having been totally ineffective, but they had both enjoyed half-a-dozen marvellous holidays at the sponsor's expense.

Money, if it is available, can of course buy help, particularly in the first few months when an extra pair of hands can be invaluable. One financial advantage of having twins is that they qualify immediately for family allowances, which are only payable after the birth of the second child. Two children's allowances can be claimed against income tax and, of course, the double maternity grant (£25 per child) is payable to every twin mother. But there are no bounties, no prizes and no financial rewards for fecundity.

Until 1957, mothers of triplets or more, were entitled to Queen Anne's Bounty worth £1 per child. Although this custom has disappeared, any such mother wanting a royal stamp of approval, can get a message of congratulations from the Queen by writing to the Privy Purse Office at Buckingham Palace.

The all-time record for such productivity, as stated in *The*

Guinness Book of Records, was achieved by a Russian peasant who in 27 births, produced 16 pairs of twins, 7 sets of triplets and 4 lots of quads. She lived from 1816 to 1872 and her fame was such that she was presented at the court of Tsar Alexander II. However proud she may have been, the poor woman will no doubt have had problems in making ends meet with such an enormous family. Even if it had existed, it is unlikely that any insurance company would have given her the time of day. Nowadays, it is not only possible but advisable to insure against twins, provided it is done in good time. It does not cost much and can provide a very useful buffer against any resultant financial strain. Lloyds under-writers are the chief insurers and their proposal forms are obtainable from any good insurance broker.

It is better to set the wheels in motion sooner rather than later: $3\frac{1}{2}$ months' pregnancy is the deadline and, depending on the amount of cover required, it may take time to find different companies to share the risk. The premium is determined by the family history of both husband and wife as well as the maternal age. The starting rate for a woman under 30 with no twins in the family tree, is likely to be £2.50 for each £100 paid out. It will increase to $3–3\frac{1}{2}$ per cent between the ages of 30 and 35 and, if there are previous twins or close relatives have them, the premium can rise to 10 per cent.

Lloyds reckon that half the policies on which they pay out come from people with no history of twins. But the other half do have the cards stacked against them, so whichever category fits there is a lot to be said in favour of taking out insurance.

The usual policy, known in the trade as a layette policy, is for a couple of hundred pounds to cover the initial expenditure of bringing two into the world. At one time, Lloyds took a very moral stand and felt that such insurance should definitely not be regarded as a flutter; nor would they insure for very large sums. Now, however, it is possible to insure for as much as £5,000—enough to pay for private education, perhaps, or the extra help that may be desirable. A gamble? Not according to one grandmother who insured her pregnant daughter with the words: 'I don't smoke, I don't drink and I don't gamble. But if you have another set of twins, you will have to move to a bigger house and you will need help.' Insure she did, at 9 per cent, and when a second set of twins were born the grandmother's foresight enabled the young couple to build an extra floor on to their house, which they would not have been able to do otherwise.

Before the proposal form is accepted, the insurers require medical confirmation of the date on which the birth is expected. To cover themselves against any premeditated mistake over the true commencement of the pregnancy, the insurance companies specify that they will not pay if the twins are born more than six weeks before the specified date. In practice, they will examine sympathetically any claim for premature twins, if their birthweight bears out that they are indeed premature. However, as nothing on the proposal form indicates that such a claim may be paid, it does seem rather unjust since some potential claimants will never claim and others might worry themselves into giving birth prematurely just because of that clause.

Certainly any treatment designed to increase fertility would cancel the policy as would any medical opinion expressed before the policy was taken out that a multiple birth could be expected.

Once the policy has been taken out, there is no more to do than to sit back and wait for the birth. If more than one is born, after confirmation that they have had a separate existence from their mother for at least twenty-four hours, you just wait for the cheque to come. If triplets or quads are born, the amount payable is doubled.

3 Diagnosis in Duplicate

The discovery that twins are on the way is likely to occur in the last few weeks of pregnancy. It is, however, possible that nobody has suspected the presence of twins until after the first baby has been born when, surprise, surprise, a second one is found to be waiting to put in an appearance.

Whether a diagnosis is made to establish if a pregnant woman is carrying more than one baby depends almost entirely on whether anyone examining her has had reason to suspect this. Several factors would arouse such suspicion. The size of the uterus would be one. If this is found to be greater than warranted for the stage of pregnancy, it could mean twins. If there is more fluid than usual in the uterus, that could be another indication. An obvious pointer would be if more than one baby can be felt. Conversely, if the doctor is unable to feel the baby, that can be a sign that there is a crowd in there. Even the humble tape measure can yield valuable information. Used to measure the bulge, experience will tell the doctor that, if the number of inches around the middle is greater than would be expected at that date, a couple of babies may be on the way. Lastly, if the doctor has a puzzled look on his face as he carries out his examination and if he tells you that he cannot decide whether he is feeling one head and one bottom or two heads, you can be sure of getting a note sending you to hospital for confirmation.

The diagnosis of twins is normally confirmed with the aid of X-rays or Ultra Sound machines. Where this relatively new equipment is available, Ultra Sound will be used. It works on similar principles to radar, sending out high frequency sound waves, which are reflected as echoes from the surfaces of various organs, such as the womb, the baby's

37

head or the placenta. The resulting pattern shows up on a screen and can be interpreted by the doctor as different internal objects and, in particular, whether more than one foetus is present.

Diagnosis by Ultra Sound is completely painless. The patient lies down on her back on a couch in a darkened room. The arm of the machine has something resembling a microphone attached to it and moves over her stomach, which has been previously rubbed with oil. The visual representation of the resulting sound waves shows up on the screen by her side and, with the help of the doctor, the patient can see for herself what is going on inside her. If she asks nicely, she may even be given a print to take home and stick on the first page of her babies' photo album!

Ultra Sound for diagnostic purposes has no harmful effect on the unborn child and, although not normally used until the 28th week of pregnancy, it can be employed as early as the 7th or 8th week. This can be valuable, as Ultra Sound can also establish the position of the placenta and measure the rate of growth of the foetus.

Where Ultra Sound machines are not available, X-rays will be taken between the 26th and 28th week. X-rays are reasonably accurate, but not completely foolproof. If the baby moves while the X-ray is being exposed, this can blur out his shadow and thereby make his presence more difficult to detect. However, X-rays do tell you more or less conclusively what you are harbouring.

In order to have this kind of diagnostic X-ray, the pregnant woman does the seemingly impossible. She lies face down on a bed cushioned with plastic foam padding and remains still for the time it takes to expose the photo. The idea of lying on your stomach, however briefly, when seven months' pregnant, may seem a physical impossibility, but it isn't. It is simply a question of mind over matter and a great deal of matter at that!

There are other ways of trying to establish whether there

is more than one baby lurking around inside, but they are fairly inconclusive. Listening to the foetal heartbeats is one method, but here it is necessary for two doctors to listen simultaneously and count aloud. If the counts do not coincide, this is proof of two separate hearts beating. However, as women who have already had a baby will know, the foetal heartbeat is not always easily audible. It can be heard most readily through the baby's back. If one of the twins is lying differently, his heartbeat may therefore remain undetected.

Trying to diagnose twins by touch alone may indicate the presence of either one extremely lively infant or perhaps two or a multiplicity of foetal parts.

Although we rightly put our trust in the medical profession in all that concerns our bodies, it would be wrong to ignore our own feelings in the matter. After all, a pregnant woman is not only wrapped up in her unborn child but wrapped around it. She is, therefore, more acutely conscious of its movements and its life in her womb than any outsider, however great his expertise may be. If she has had a baby before, she may well decide that, unlike her last pregnancy, there is a small stampede going on inside her. One mother spoke of having felt eight distinct movements long before anyone else suspected twins. Another, equally convinced that she was expecting twins, had the greatest difficulty in persuading the hospital to try and find out. At first, this mother-to-be was dismissed as hysterical, but finally they X-rayed her and then when they looked at the plate had some doubt as to whether there were two or three babies.

Even mothers in their first pregnancy frequently question their more experienced friends as to whether they too could feel so much movement inside. There are other warning signs which often, although not always, arouse a pregnant woman's suspicions or should be heeded.

If you are sternly told that you are putting on too much weight and should stop stuffing yourself with cream buns, when you know this to be an absolute slander, twins may be the cause. If in the first three months of pregnancy your friends look at you in disbelief when you claim that you have six months to go, that could also make you think twice.

There is a reasonable chance that suspicions about the presence of a second baby will be confirmed or rejected by subsequent medical investigation. However, an overall figure for England and Wales would show that about 15 per cent of all multiple births remain undetected before the birth. But this figure will vary radically from one hospital to another. Given a highly skilled teaching hospital, far fewer twins will slip through the diagnostic net than perhaps in a small cottage hospital which has less specialised staff and a much smaller number of maternity cases passing through it. In the latter, the number of unexpected twin births may be much higher than the national average.

Several factors may contribute to surprise all round in the delivery room. Obese women are much more likely to escape detection; the extra layer of fat can effectively disguise twins. Just as a pebble is less discernible under a thick blanket than under a sheet, so bumps in the stomach are well camouflaged under too much natural padding. Increased measurements or weight are also not so easily detected. Since there is no reason for a doctor to look for twins unless he thinks they might be there, plump ladies are more likely to harbour unsuspected twins.

Another factor is failure of the mother to attend an ante-natal clinic. If she does not bother to have regular check-ups and is admitted to hospital in labour at the last moment, obviously nobody has had a chance to assess the situation. Then again, according to the medical profession, women are notoriously bad at knowing exactly when their last period occurred. Confronted with a patient's notes which specify, for instance, that her last period occurred twelve weeks before, and after an examination which corresponds more or less with what would be expected at this stage, the doctor has no reason to question his findings.

Much depends on the degree of experience of the examining doctor. A practitioner who, over a lengthy period, has examined seventy-nine pregnant women, each of whom has given birth to one baby, is perhaps less likely to realise that the eightieth is harbouring twins than his counterpart in a busy maternity clinic, through whose doors hundreds or thousands of pregnant women pass every year. In such a clinic, a doctor would not only have all his own patients to examine but would be called upon by colleagues to give a second opinion.

The counterpart to undetected twins is, of course, when everyone confidently predicts that twins are on the way and everyone is proved wrong. Judging by the number of women to whom this has happened, it would seem that such inaccurate forecasts occur much more frequently than an actual twin birth, whether it takes place with or without prior warning.

If the diagnosis is positive, it is common practice nowadays for women expecting more than one baby to come into hospital for rest at about twenty-eight weeks. The stay may vary between two and four weeks and it is very important to comply with this arrangement, however difficult it may be for you to do so.

This prescribed hospital stay is not intended as a lovely rest for the mother, who may indeed feel perfectly fit and raring to go, but as an invaluable insurance that the twins are born at the best moment and with the best chance of a healthy life.

The reason why doctors try to establish by the 28th week of pregnancy whether a multiple birth is expected, is because in such a case the woman is more likely to go into premature labour between the 28th and 36th week thereby putting the babies at risk. Medical evidence shows that, by resting in bed, the danger of going into labour too early is reduced considerably. Furthermore, toxaemia, which can include high blood pressure, protein in the urine and swelling of the fingers and ankles, and which occurs in 5–10 per cent of single pregnancies—is three times as frequent in twin pregnancies.

Many doctors would, no doubt, be satisfied to let mothers-to-be stay at home, if they could ensure that they remained in bed during the danger period. Most women, however, find it difficult if not impossible to be in their own home and stay firmly put in bed when they are not actually ill and may, on the contrary, feel extremely well. The urge to potter around, tidy up, rearrange the furniture, cook ahead or pop out to do a little shopping is irresistible, and with other children around bed rest is out of the question unless some-one else is present to replace the mother. If there are young children at home, a lengthy separation is obviously not desirable. An increasing number of hospitals allow children to visit their mothers and, if there is a choice of hospitals, it is not a bad idea to try to find out in advance what attitudes and rules prevail regarding visiting at different hospitals.

While lying in bed and perhaps contemplating your navel, you may find that it is becoming increasingly difficult to catch sight of. You may also wonder whether you will ever be able to get into your normal clothes after the event. Two babies take up more room and, as stomach muscles have to stretch farther to accommodate them, it may take longer for these to tighten up again. Provided the doctor is in agreement—and he must be consulted—muscles can be kept in tone before the birth by practising pulling in the tummy. It used to be thought that rubbing with oil would prevent stretch marks, but this is now considered a myth. Some women get them, others don't. But oil may prevent the itchiness which may be caused by tautly stretched skin.

Hospital rest can pass very pleasantly and it may well be the last stretch of completely free time, totally without duties or responsibilities that a mother will have for some years to come. Apart from routine tests and examinations, nothing will be done medically unless there is any condition which requires treatment. If the twins are the first babies, then all you have to do is to move in with a few good books, your prettiest nighties, dressing gown and slippers, and relax.

4 Taking Delivery

The same kid twice

Dennis the Menace

Twins should be born in hospital, preferably one with a good obstetric department. Only a hospital will have the necessary equipment, medical staff and knowledge to cope with every eventuality as a matter of routine. If a home confinement had been envisaged, once it is known that there is to be more than one baby, this plan must be changed.

Greatly improved antenatal care and obstetric knowledge has enormously reduced infant mortality during this century. While more twins survive birth than used to be the case, they are nevertheless more vulnerable before, during and immediately after birth, and the risks are minimised in hospital.

Two of the main preoccupations of hospital doctors will be to determine the best moment for the babies' arrival and to control the interval between the two births. The right moment for a baby to be born is when it has reached a degree of maturity which enables it to exist outside the womb. A baby born well ahead of term is judged to be premature, with a definite correlation between its weight and the degree of maturity. The mean gestation period for a single baby is 40 weeks with an average weight of 7lb at birth, but gestation for twins is normally 37 weeks with a mean weight of 5lb per baby and slightly lower weights for twins of the same sex—which, of course, includes all identicals. Thirty-five weeks of pregnancy is normal for triplets with birth-weights of 4lb each and for quads the average is 34 weeks with weights of 3lb.

However, because the lower birth-weight for multiples

44

is normal, this should not be equated with the same weight occurring in singles. For example, there is a lower rate of infant mortality in twins weighing under $5\frac{1}{2}$lb than in singles of that weight; the reason put forward is that a single baby weighing less than $5\frac{1}{2}$lb is more likely to have medical problems which have retarded his growth. Conversely, while single babies weighing over 8lb are more vulnerable, with twins the risk begins at 7lb. Exactly what causes the lower birth-weight in twins is not known, but it may be that the uterus is unable to contain more than about 12lb of baby without starting to contract.

In the event, doctors have to judge the best moment between too low and too high a birth-weight, although the second alternative is less likely to arise, since twins are normally born before term. When this stage has been reached, the pregnancy is sufficiently advanced and there is no sign of labour in the offing, the doctors may consider it necessary to induce labour by breaking the membranes. However much a mother may prefer a completely natural childbirth, with as little medical intervention as possible, she should remember that such an induction—also called breaking the waters—is not due to medical flights of fancy but to sound obstetric principles, designed to ensure the delivery of healthy babies.

It could even happen that, where there is a shortage of hospital staff, a baby is induced so that it can be delivered when there are enough people around to provide optimum conditions. Such reasons may be regrettable but, since they are put into operation for the benefit of the mother and baby, they must, nevertheless, be considered valid.

The first stage of labour is the same whether one or more babies are due. But once you get to action stations in the delivery room, you may face one phenomenon about which few hospitals take the trouble to warn you. It has been the experience of numerous mothers-to-be that the delivery room suddenly fills up with an astonishing number of people.

Gowned and masked, the patient may well be alarmed and wonder what medical complications are anticipated. The simple fact is that twin births are of great interest, medically speaking, and anyone on the wards not otherwise engaged comes to watch and learn. A few words to the star of this performance, the mother, would not come amiss. After all, when a very private affair turns into a box-office sell-out, she is entitled to know why. Still, star treatment is also awarded from a medical point of view. Whereas straight-forward single births may be supervised by a relatively junior houseman, twins merit greater obstetric experience and skill and a senior doctor or consultant will do the delivering.

The length of labour is not normally any longer for twins than for singles. The position of the foetuses will have been established before birth. In single births, 96 per cent are vertex (head down). With twins, approximate figures show that in 47 per cent of cases both babies are vertex; in 37 per cent one is vertex and the other breech, in 8–9 per cent both are breech; in 5 per cent one is vertex and one lying crossways, and in 2 per cent one is breech and the other lying crossways. Where there is one vertex and one breech, the vertex one is delivered first about one and a half times as often; and if one is lying vertically (head up or down) and the other across, the vertical twin is eight times more likely to be born first.

Once the first baby is delivered, it is common practice to ensure that the second one is born within about fifteen minutes. This may mean medical intervention so that the interval between the two births does not become more lengthy. The reason why nature is frequently not allowed to run its course and let the second baby be born spontaneously is partly because the placenta may separate after the first birth and the second twin could be short of oxygen. He should therefore be delivered at the optimum time.

Although 5lb is a normal weight for each twin, considerable variations are by no means unknown. According to *The*

Guinness Book of Records, the heaviest surviving twins, born in the United States in 1924, were a boy and a girl weighing 14lb and 13lb 12oz respectively. At the other end of the scale, two surviving baby girls born in Peterborough in 1931 weighed 16oz and 19oz each. Recent research shows that twins tend to be not only lighter but slightly shorter at birth than singles, although this normally evens out.

Apart from the medical skills required to help bring healthy babies into the world, a sympathetic and supportive attitude on the part of the nursing staff can do much to enhance the mother's stay in hospital. Those women whose only wish is for the next birth to take place at home, surrounded by their family and without the rules and restrictions of a hospital ward, are those whose stay has been unhappy. New mothers are often highly emotional creatures, perhaps lacking self-confidence and much in need of moral support. Some women feel strongly that the only nurses to staff maternity wards should be mothers themselves, who will be more sympathetic in that they have undergone the same experience of birth. As it is, a few nurses are disdainful of maternity work, feeling that it does not make use of their real medical skills, an attitude which can be upsetting to new mothers who may be perfectly well physically but emotionally vulnerable.

At no time is the encouraging—or alternatively the unsympathetic—attitude of the nurses more keenly felt than when it comes to feeding the babies. Most mothers have fairly strong feelings, either in favour or against breastfeeding. Quite a few find that their views are not taken into consideration, particularly if they do not happen to fall into line with what the nurses say 'We always do here'. Mothers who do not want to breastfeed are occasionally browbeaten into doing so against their natural inclinations, while others, desperately wanting to do so, find that their babies are getting extra bottles in the nursery, which are bound to take the edge off their appetite when the mother gives them the breast.

No amount of will power can establish a good milk supply if there is not enough sucking to get it going. Provided there are no physical or medical problems involved, it is the mother's inalienable right to choose the method whereby she feeds her babies and she should hold out for what she wants. Obviously she must be guided by the medical staff, if they feel that her babies are not thriving. The will to breastfeed is not always enough to make it a possibility and some mothers can make themselves ill, as well as depriving their infants of essential nourishment, if they persist in trying when it is not going to work; and twins do require a more plentiful milk supply than perhaps they can provide.

Before deciding on the method of feeding to be adopted, certain factors should be considered which might affect your choice. Breastfeeding the twins will effectively manacle the mother to one place, and when she returns home she may find it difficult to attend to other young children while she has two at the breast. It may, therefore, in some circumstances be more expedient to bottlefeed. However, if she has to prepare separate bottles for each feed and there is no refrigerator in which to store a twenty-four hour batch made up once a day, breastfeeding will save her time and work, as well as, of course, costing nothing.

Whether the babies are breastfed or bottlefed, some hospitals recommend giving a bottle of boiled water and glucose at 2 am from birth. Provided medical advisers agree, this is an excellent arrangement since many babies find it sufficiently comforting to stop crying but not rewarding enough to make them wake up specially for it. This bottle frequently weans them off the 2 am feed which, from the mother's point of view, is the one she feels least like waking up for. It also means that if the babies do wake up, her husband can take his turn with some nocturnal feeding.

However cocooned the twins may be when they arrive for feeding and provided there is no medical reason why you should not do so, undress them and look at them properly, individually and together. Every parent has a lurking fear that a baby may not be normal and it is only by examining every part of each twin that this fear is dispelled. At birth, each will have had a tape fastened around an ankle or a wrist, bearing a legend such as Smith I and Smith II. However quickly the mother reckons that she can tell them apart, it is advisable to retain those tapes until some time after discharge from hospital, when the father is as certain of their identity as she is. Otherwise, there may always be an element of doubt. It may not be particularly important unless the babies happen to be of royal blood, or the eldest is destined to succeed to an earldom or a fortune is at stake. Still, not only the parents but the children too have a right to know which is the first born.

Having visitors after the event is something every mother enjoys but too many of them can be tiring. Frequent visits by individuals are better than four visitors at a time twice a week. Patients are happiest in hospitals with fairly free visiting hours but where the number of visitors present at any one time is limited. If there are other children who need reassurance that their mother has not left for good, hopefully she will be in a hospital which allows them to visit her, but they should not stay too long nor start turning somersaults on her bed! Not only the mother but the woman in the next bed may find it too much.

The length of the hospital stay will depend on the health of the mother and the babies and also on the shortage of beds. Ten days is average. If the babies are premature, they may be kept longer than their mother, who will be able to spend time with them every day.

All mothers know the date of their children's birth and their weight. Most will remember the interval between the births but the Registrar General makes allowance for forgetfulness by insisting on the inclusion of the time of birth on their birth certificates. The hospital will provide a note of each baby's height too, if asked.

In the interest of regaining a trim figure as quickly as possible, post-natal exercises can be started almost immediately after the birth, provided this has not required forceps or a Caesarian. A few lucky women snap back into shape almost immediately without doing much to help their muscles along. The rest have to work at it. Anyone who has attended ante-natal relaxation classes will know the drill already and others will automatically be visited by the hospital's physiotherapist after the birth. For those who have not received instructions regarding the exercises to be done, two useful leaflets provide all the necessary information. They are *Your Baby and Your Figure* by L. Burns, published by Churchill Livingstone and available from bookshops, and *Keeping Fit for Pregnancy and Labour* by Margaret Williams, which can be obtained from the National Childbirth Trust, 9 Queensborough Terrace, London W2. It does not pay to neglect these exercises and ten minutes set aside each day is all that is needed to ensure that the body regains its suppleness and that clothes fit again.

5 The Twins at Home

Twenty tiny fingers
Twenty tiny toes
Two angel faces
Each with a turned up nose

Francis Day and Hunter

The very fact of being home again, within your own four walls, will be reassuring and, in the first few weeks or months, the babies' needs are easily satisfied, even if they lack patience once they have voiced their demands. Food and sleep, a change of nappies when indicated, clean skin and clean clothes, fresh air and plenty of love is all that's required at first.

FEEDING

Feeding the twins will take up a lot of time at the beginning, but as they and their needs become more familiar, a predictable pattern will emerge and feeds will settle down to a peaceful and happy routine. In hospital, a nurse will undoubtedly have helped the mother with breastfeeding, handing her the babies when she is comfortably installed in bed and ready to start. If there is someone around at home who can do this for the first few weeks, it is a great help. It makes life easier until the mother has got the hang of it and can manage by herself.

Although people without twin experience are surprisingly unimaginative when it comes to figuring out how it is possible to breastfeed twins simultaneously, it is a very simple procedure which, if it works, works beautifully. What happens is this: the mother installs herself on a bed or divan and puts a cushion or pillow on her lap. She then places the

babies, with their heads cradled in her hands, on the pillow, with their legs tucked under her arm. The babies' heads are then lifted up so that they can suck. No changing over is necessary since, provided they have roughly equal appetites, supply and demand will be the same. Newborn babies are lightweights and continue to be easily manoeuvrable for quite a few weeks. Therefore, even if one needs attention while the other continues to suck, it presents no difficulties. The mother can also raise the pillow with her knees, enabling her to have both hands free while the baby continues to feed undisturbed.

When it is time to bring up their wind, it is quite easy for her to hoist both babies up on to her shoulders and, with arms crossed, pat each on the back until the required burp is heard. Alternatively, one or both can be placed on their fronts on her lap to bring up their wind.

Many mothers enjoy breastfeeding twins and succeed admirably. However, it is particularly important for mothers of twins to feel well and have plenty of energy, as they will have more to do. If, therefore, breastfeeding tires you, it is much better to switch to bottles rather than risk exhaustion.

Nor should an inability to breastfeed, or taking advice not to, be equated with failure as a woman; that is as logical as feeling guilty about having blonde hair!

If and when the twins are on bottles, it saves time and labour if a batch of feeds, sufficient for one day, is made up at the same time and stored in the refrigerator. If there is no cold store, this procedure would not be safe. Tinned milk is much easier and quicker than dried milk to mix and make up. Although slightly more expensive, it does not have the awful smell of dried milk, nor does it leave scum around the inside of bottles, making them so difficult to clean.

The preparation of the bottles should be done at a time of day when there is peace and no other demands are likely to be made. Interruptions can make for constant recounts in the number of scoops and ounces which have to be measured accurately. The evening may be the best time and, furthermore, this is a job which the husband may be quite happy to undertake.

Bottlefeeding, can also be done simultaneously, by cradling one baby in the crook of one arm with a bottle held in the same hand and the second baby stretched out by the mother's side on a pillow, fed with a bottle in her other hand. Alternatively, reclining baby chairs can be used; with the babies strapped in, the mother is free to sit in front of them

on the floor, or, if she puts them on a table, she can sit on a chair in front of them with a bottle in each hand.

If the babies are fed in their chairs, each one will have to be burped in turn and, because this is a rather impersonal way of feeding, the mother will undoubtedly want to make up for the lack of physical contact by giving each baby extra amounts of individual cuddling and loving; these are just as necessary for his wellbeing as milk.

It is better to rinse the bottles straight away, to avoid real scrubbing later when the milk has dried. After washing, leave them in a bucket of sterilising solution until the next day when they can be rinsed under clean water and a fresh batch made up. Today's bottle solution can then become tomorrow's nappy-bucket steriliser, with the water from one bucket being poured into the other—but do not put the nappies in the bottle container!

When another person is present at feeding times, let him or her feed one baby while you feed the other. It makes life easier. However, if this happens regularly, make sure you feed each baby in turn. One grown-up twin remembers that his mother's sister, who lived with them at first, used to feed him all the time while his mother fed his twin. For some years he was always known as 'Auntie's baby' which not surprisingly both confused and riled him. A helping hand can cause problems if, as sometimes happens, one of the babies screeches the moment a strange face appears on the horizon. In such cases it is best to play it by ear and steer an even course between upsetting the timid baby and always handing the uncomplaining one to others.

These methods of feeding in the first few months are fairly straightforward when the twins are evenly matched for appetite and frequency of feeds. What if there is a big discrepancy in weight? If one twin should need feeding every three hours initially—and it does not happen very often—then he will just have to be given food more frequently, although it may be possible to feed both together every second or third feed. A much more likely possibility is that one will wake up hungry earlier than the other. Whether a baby is fed on demand or kept on a strict schedule is a matter for the mother to decide. One mother to whom I talked thrived on time tables. She even set the alarm clock at 2 am when she and the nanny, who was present for the first year, got up, actually dressed and prepared and gave feeds, while her husband also came down to make hot drinks for the adults. For those who feel like a party in the middle of the night, this is no doubt a good plan, but most of us hope fervently that the babies' in-built alarm clock will fail to ring so that we can remain in our warm beds.

Much depends on other commitments as well as personal

feelings in shaping the feeding routine or lack of it during the day. If there is a meal to get ready for other members of the family or an early night is desirable, it is better to choose the time for feeding the twins rather than have it imposed on you. If feeding on demand is more to your liking but you do not want to spend all day giving feeds, it makes sense to feed both twins when the first one wakes up hungry. If they are always fed in sequence, it is all too easy to spend most of the day with a bottle in your hand or a breast at the ready. It is also surprisingly easy to forget which twin had the last feed and which one is entitled to one immediately if not sooner. The only solution to that problem is to have a blackboard in their room on which to chalk up each mission completed and for whom.

Feeding times should be peaceful, relaxed and contented. To make them so, it is important to have everything to hand, such as tissues and bottle warmers, as one cannot get up and move around with two babies. One should also forestall any interruptions for the same reason. If there is nobody else around to answer the telephone, take it off the hook; warn regular callers that this is what you will do so that they do not ring the operator to complain that your line is out of order. If friends tend to drop in for a coffee when you have just stripped for action, either arrange to leave the door on the latch or get them to time their arrival so that you can open the door at a convenient moment.

One mother found feeding times ideal for reading although turning the pages can be difficult. Others listen to the radio; but soft harmonious music or low pitched talks are more conducive to peaceful babies than martial music and melodrama. Most mothers require no outside stimulus, finding the time spent at very close quarters with their babies when they are contented and highly receptive to her completely engrossing and rewarding. It is a time for contemplation, for relaxed enjoyment of the threesome, for getting to know each other. It should not be a time for worrying about the washing up or the shopping or the letters which remain unanswered. Babies are very sensitive to moods and anxieties in their mother, so it is worth putting all cares out of your mind and concentrating on the job in hand.

When the time comes for the introduction of solids into the twins' diet, make it easy for yourself. Cut corners where they can be cut without harm to anyone. Bought baby foods are a great boon as time savers. Anyone who hints, as a health visitor did to one mother, that you are neglecting your maternal responsibilities by not cooking and mashing non-stop, should be given short shrift and perhaps the gentle admonition that she might change places with you for a few days.

In the first months, infants have tiny appetites as far as solids are concerned. The time spent preparing minute portions is disproportionate to the quantity required. Nor is much money likely to be saved, if one counts the cost of fuel for cooking plus the waste of what gets thrown away. Obviously, mashing half a banana is just as quick and cheap as a tinned alternative, but the main principle, at the beginning, is to suit yourself.

As the babies' appetites grow and they get through more than a tin per meal, it will become worthwhile preparing meals for them yourself. With a blender, whether electric or manual, the mincing and mashing becomes child's play. It is often almost as quick and certainly cheaper to cook large quantities; for instance, stewed fruit, milk puddings and vegetables can be prepared in sufficient quantities to feed the children at lunchtime and the adults at dinner. It may not be the *haute cuisine* your husband has been lucky enough to get in the past, but the addition of a few adult ingredients like wine in the stew and herbs on the vegetables can quickly turn baby pap into lovely time-saving meals for the parents.

Once solids are introduced into the diet, the golden rule is to use one bowl and one spoon until the babies can begin to feed themselves. They will catch each other's germs anyhow and there are no advantages in each having his own feeding utensils. It just entails more washing up and, unless you are ambidextrous, it is awkward to use both hands or to offer alternate spoons. It is not necessary to decant the baby food into a different container if it comes in a glass jar or tin. Aesthetic considerations aside, the food can be heated up in its original container, well stirred to ensure that no part is too hot or too cold and fed straight into the waiting mouths. There is less waste that way too.

For any middle-of-the-night feeding, much time and chilly padding around the house is saved by having two electric bottle warmers in the nursery. Alternatively, a plastic container holding the bottles, to which you add hot water from a vacuum flask filled in the evening or from an electric kettle, speeds up the preparation for this most unwelcome nocturnal interlude.

SLEEP

Apart from food, sleep is the main factor in a baby's life and it is in the mother's interests to ensure sound sleep for her twins.

It is normal to put both in the same room for the first years anyway, even if they could have separate rooms. It is very rare for one to wake the other when it cries. Separate cribs right from the start are best. The old-fashioned way used to be to have one at each end of a large cot but, apart from the fact that two newborn infants look completely lost even in an area 4ft by 2ft, they will not stay at their appointed ends for long. Babies are more mobile from the word go than might be thought. Try putting one on his tummy, place your hand across the soles of his feet and watch him start to crawl.

Having two in the same cot also makes it psychologically more difficult to attend to only one. One mother who tried it found that, when one cried, she felt obliged to pick the second one up too, even when he was sleeping soundly. After giving each twin his own cot, she could let sleeping babies lie.

There is no need to buy two cribs, particularly if money is tight, which it usually is. A pram can double as a crib, provided it is always dry. A second pram for naps in the garden will be invaluable later on, and until it is needed there it can serve as a crib for one baby. Many families keep carrycots and prams for some time after they are needed, in case there are any more arrivals. As they take up valuable storage space, friends and neighbours are often delighted to lend you what is needed. For all that, look gift horses in the mouth if you don't want to be lumbered with white elephants. One mother was given a double carrycot which, apart from resembling a small coffin, was too heavy and unwieldy for one person to carry and too large to put in the back of anything other than a van. Another got a lovely twin pram which was too wide to go through the back door into the garden.

Since babies outgrow their first cribs in three to four months, it is pointless to spend a lot of money at this stage; even a drawer out of a chest of drawers, if suitably padded, can serve quite adequately in an emergency.

The room in which the babies sleep need be no different from any room suitable for a nursery—with one exception: it must be big enough to accommodate not only two cribs but later on two cots and then two beds, unless the twins are moved to separate rooms as they grow older. Babies are often given the smallest bedroom, which in many houses is really a box room and much too small to accommodate two children. Babies grow fast into creatures who crawl around the floor, playing with bricks and stacking beakers and soft toys. If there is no room to set aside as a playroom and you don't want your living room cluttered up with toys, it may be a good idea from the start to allot a room in which the twins can sleep and play for years to come. Often the parents' bedroom is the biggest and a swop could be considered; after all, it is usually totally unused except at night. A big room for the twins can also contain a divan for the mother's use when feeding or resting, or on those occasions when one of the babies is teething or fretful and needs frequent comforting during the night.

It should be borne in mind that small children are unwilling to play out of view and earshot of their mother. Up to the age of three anyway, you have to be prepared to stay with them in the room of your choice because if Mahomet won't come to the mountain, the mountain will come to Mahomet. Their beautiful, spacious nursery will remain empty as toy cars and bricks are carted into the living-room or kitchen or wherever you happen to be.

Apart from the resulting mess, safety must be taken into consideration. When little creatures are crawling around the floor and grabbing everything in sight, it is much better to forget the cooking and the housework and stay with them in their room rather than in the kitchen which is rarely safe. Twins' playtime is fun and, if they do not require non-stop participation in their games, you can always write letters, read, do a crossword puzzle or some mending. One mother used this time to knit for the whole family, which she would otherwise not have had either the time or inclination to do.

Newborn babies sleep most of the time and, since their mother's wellbeing and, by extension, their own depends to a large degree on how much rest she gets, it cannot be stressed too strongly that a new mother of twins should seize the opportunity to put her feet up at least once a day. That applies equally if she already has other children; although the experienced mother, even if kept busier, will probably be able to take the twins more in her stride than a new and inexperienced mother. With no other children clamouring for attention, a mother should be able to take a nap when the babies are having theirs. The best time is after the 2 pm feed. One mother took the precaution of pinning a note to her front door saying 'No callers until 3.30' to ward off well-wishers and friends eager to pop in and look at the babies. People understand and do not take offence.

It is a heartening fact that, according to recent research, mothers of twins do not lose more sleep than those who produce singly; on average, they have just ten minutes less sleep per night when the babies are six months old. However, with too little rest, mothers of twins can become very tired and find it difficult to cope. A helpful husband is about the best insurance against lack of sleep at night. If he takes his turn to get up and settle a fretful baby or give a bottle, the mother is much more likely to manage well during the day.

Unlike their parents, babies do not differentiate much between day and night, but for the mother there is a difference between the twins' night-time sleep and their day-time naps. Many feel that the children sleep that much better for being out in the fresh air during the day. It is advisable though to put each baby in a separate pram from the time they are a couple of months old, otherwise they will kick each other awake. There is no twin pram big enough to allow two of them to lie stretched out. If there is no accessible garden or balcony, and the mother just does not feel up to getting the twins ready to go out, they will do just as well—providing they are suitably dressed and there is no draught—if they are left in their cots which have been pushed near to the open window.

What should be done if they don't sleep when they are supposed to? The fact that they are twins will not make them do everything simultaneously. If one cries and the other does not, what then? If it is a cry of hunger, feed both. If it is for any other reason, just see to the baby who requires attention. Change his nappies, burp him, rock him, cuddle him. Don't feel compelled to pick up the other one unless he is wide awake and just too polite to make it known that he also wants a kiss and a cuddle.

For the constant grouch, the twin who will not settle even after the mother has satisfied herself that nothing ails him and everything else has been tried, give him a dummy. A dummy is a highly emotive concept, violently rejected by many mothers, and it is certainly neither attractive nor hygienic. If it does the trick, however, it may be better to sublimate any aesthetic considerations in favour of silence in the nursery. Millions of mothers have found dummies a godsend; they should never, of course, be dipped in syrup or fruit juice to make them more palatable, as this will attack the teeth before they have even been cut.

With luck, good sleeping habits are quickly established and while the babies sleep their mother is free—free at night to sleep herself and free during the day to attend to other matters or to rest.

BATH TIME

Babies have to be kept clean and most people have the idea that a daily bath is a ritual not to be neglected. It is not true. Nearly every mother of twins to whom I have spoken kept them spick and span with a bath every second day, either bathing both together every other day or one each day, and it has not done them any harm.

Baby books frequently direct mothers to a time before the 10 am feed as the hallowed moment for such ablutions. It may indeed be convenient for many mothers but, if it does not happen to be a good time for you, feel free to choose one that suits you better, as long as it is before a feed and not after, when contented, replete babies are sleepy. Many fathers particularly enjoy their children's bathtime, so the evening, when they can watch or participate, may be the most relaxed and pleasant time.

Which room is chosen for the bath depends on the home and the heating arrangements. Baby baths which have to be filled with jugs, transported from somewhere else and then emptied, can be a nuisance, particularly if the idea is to wash one baby after the other. A bath which fits over the family tub is often more practical, although it is not too

62

comfortable for the mother who has to kneel by the side. However, more unorthodox solutions should not be ruled out. One mother found the kitchen sink the ideal place. The kitchen was the warmest room in the house, the sink the right height not to give her back ache, it was easy to clean thoroughly before use and the mixer tap could be swivelled out of the way. Not perhaps what Mrs Beeton would have expected of the nursery staff, but a practical solution for some Ms 1970!

While the babies have to be supported in the bath, ie before they are able to sit up and remain sitting steadily, they must be bathed separately. Once they can sit safely and unsupported, they can graduate to the big bath together. There they will be accompanied by an armada of plastic boats and a school of fish to replace those shelves laden with bottles of bath salts, trailing plants or other more trendy images which fond parents may have previously tried to introduce. Of course, no toddler is left in the bath without an adult present. If the telephone rings and there is no one else to answer it, just forget it; by the time the babies have been taken out of the water, dried and put in a safe place, it will have stopped ringing anyway.

NAPPY CHANGING

Even without a daily bath, the babies will, of course, be topped and tailed whenever necessary and, for this purpose, it is best to have everything ready to hand in the nursery: a bowl of fresh water, soap, cotton wool and clean towels, as well as fresh nappies, a bucket with lid for the used ones (filled with cold water to stop the aroma), safety pins, tissues, baby lotions and cream. A table or chest of drawers, suitably padded and easily wiped clean, will provide a good surface for this operation.

Wet nappies should go straight into a nappy bucket and dirty nappies should have the worst removed immediately otherwise they add to the work later. Nappy liners save a lot of unpleasant work and time in this respect.

Most mothers change nappies almost nonstop at first—every time they pick a baby up, in fact. Experience soon makes it clear when it is necessary—after the twins have been asleep for three hours and before a feed; and when it is not—namely half an hour later when they are barely damp. Mothers will also learn that, when the nappies are removed but left under the baby, there is often a repeat performance at one or both ends, which can be caught in the old nappy, thus making the whole operation more worthwhile!

When changing nappies everything that is needed should be in one place, so that there is no need to hunt for the baby lotion, which you also use to remove your make-up, or the pins which you remember putting in a pocket—but which pocket? If nappies are changed upstairs in the early morning and late afternoon, but on the sofa in the living room during the day, then keep a duplicate set of everything in a basket which can be carried around with ease. It is not an expensive indulgence because everything will get used up anyway. It will also, with a bit of luck, prevent essentials from running out unexpectedly.

LOVE AND ATTENTION

There is no timetable necessary for loving your babies and playing with them. From birth on you will want to cuddle them and talk to them. Just give in to your natural impulses and you will do the right thing. Older children must not be neglected or seem to be pushed out of the nest by their newborn siblings. It is bad enough for them to have one new brother or sister to contend with; it is adding insult to injury to be faced with two at once who cause even more comment and interest than one. It is important that the older child should not feel left out. Let him hold one of the babies when it is safe for him to do so, and give a bottle or powder a bottom if it amuses him, even if it means powder everywhere. Make time to be alone with the older child, to play with him, to read to him and to see that he has treats and outings to compensate for the cuckoos he has found in his nest and to reassure him that he has lost none of the love and attention he needs.

6 Two of Everything?

In form and feature, face and limb
I grew so like my brother
That folks got taking me for him
And each for one another

H. S. Leigh

It is a natural and desirable impulse to want to make one's children look as nice as possible and nothing looks sweeter than two beautifully dressed babies beaming out of a pram. Thank goodness, though, prettiness is no longer measured by the number of frills, little bows down the front, and miniature buttons on the cuffs of an outfit. If it were, mothers of twins would lose their sanity.

Having twins makes time-and-motion study desirable and one must learn to streamline chores as much as possible. Some routine tasks, like feeding or going out for a walk, can be done for both at the same time. Others, like bathing or dressing them must, of necessity, be a separate operation for each one. Depending on what they wear, dressing and undressing them can be quick or not.

There is a wonderful choice of delightful, colourful and practical clothes mass produced for infants and toddlers today. Apart from the normal considerations of price, suitability and style, mothers of twins should pay particular attention to the fastenings of the garments and the laundry instructions. Press studs instead of buttons or bows, envelope neck vests instead of wrap-over styles, elasticated waists instead of belts and buckles are all time-savers. Any baby clothes which are not machine washable are better not bought at all.

Synthetics and cottons will usually stand up to repeated machine washing without deterioration and it is best to

66

stick to them or to machine-washable wool. Not only is hand washing of clothes to be avoided; ironing too is an equally time-consuming and useless activity. Anything which drip-dries or tumble-dries into a reasonable finish without having to be pressed is preferable. For the busy mother, this applies not only to the twins' clothes but to her husband's shirts and anything else which must be laundered frequently.

When it comes to the actual requirements, nothing is likely to change the fact that double the normal number of items will be needed. There may come a point when the children start growing at different rates and when one may be able to wear the outgrown clothes of the other, but that is not likely to happen during the first year or so.

Except for the tiniest babies, first-size clothes are outgrown so quickly that money can be saved by either not buying them at all or only getting minimal quantities. Most mothers of twins have been astonished at the generosity of friends and relations as regards gifts of clothes, so it seems sensible to buy only the most basic layette, before the birth, adding whatever is necessary a few weeks or months later.

The first essential is, of course, nappies. They are a major investment nowadays but it is a false economy to buy too few. Six dozen would be ideal for twins; although, depending on the washing and particularly the drying facilities available, four dozen might be sufficient, but nothing is worse than waiting for damp nappies to dry, with none in reserve. Switching on fires to speed up the drying costs money which would be better spent on buying more nappies.

Nappies are available square or shaped—the former more adaptable, the latter neater. Individual preference, as well as advice from other mothers, will help you choose. Nappy liners are inexpensive and save a great deal of work. Wet strength paper tissues also do a good job and are cheaper. Disposable nappies, while fine for later on, are not usually considered suitable for a newborn baby—nor are they always 'disposable'. One young family with twins spent a week's holiday in a beautiful old cottage. To their horror, the lavatory became blocked up by such nappies, which entailed digging up part of the immaculate lawn in order to get at the drains. However, with due care, disposable nappies are invaluable on holiday when one wants to avoid doing more washing than necessary, for outings when carting wet nappies around is a nuisance, and for use when the washing machine breaks down at home.

Plastic pants come in all shapes and sizes. Some tie at the waist, others have press studs. Some allow the nappy to be folded inside, doing away with safety pins. Trial and error is the best way of finding out which kind are the most convenient—for you and the twins.

As regards the shopping list for clothes, to begin with there is no reason to make any distinction between day and night clothes. After all, babies are asleep either in their cots or pram and really only wake up when it is time for meals.

All-in-one stretch suits are probably the biggest boon invented, doing sterling duty twenty-four hours a day. They are decorative, cannot be kicked off and so keep the baby's feet warm; they are easy and quick to put on and take off, practical for nappy changing and emerge as new from a daily tubbing. A few of these should form the basis of every well-dressed twin's wardrobe and cut out the need for many alternative but less versatile clothes. For next-to-the-skin wear, each will need a cotton or cotton-and-wool vest, depending on the temperature. Sleeping-bags will keep them warm in cool weather on day-time pram outings, and can be substituted for blankets at night. Blankets are easily kicked off unless clips are used to anchor them in place.

The arrival of easy-care bedlinen, fitted pram and cot sheets, synthetic blankets as well as duvets, is the greatest breakthrough and reduces bedmaking to a minimum. Terylene-filled duvets are washable and therefore preferable to feather- or down-filled ones which require dry cleaning. Duvet covers can be made or bought in minimum-care fabrics and, apart from their practical qualities, at long last remove the nursery from its primrose yellow or pink aura to colours and patterns more in line with the tastes of modern mothers.

Pillows are out for infants and should not be used in prams until babies can sit up and then they should only be used when the child is actually sitting.

Layette check list

4–6 dozen nappies
6 pairs of plastic pants
6 stretch suits
6 vests
2 sleeping-bags
4 cardigans
4 bonnets
4 pairs of mittens
2 shawls
4 dresses or angel tops
4 blankets or
2 duvets with 4 covers
6 cot sheets
6 pram sheets (for 2 prams)
2 pram blankets

An important and often neglected accessory is a bib. Babies dribble and spit fairly constantly during the first couple of years; it is quicker and easier to change a bib than the whole outfit, and cuts down on laundry. Nothing smells or looks less pleasant than a baby with patches of curdled milk on his clothes. It is a good idea to buy half a dozen tough terry bibs and to use them. Forget about the tiny, dainty, embroidered ones; they may be pretty but are not practical.

As mothers of new babies are often identifiable by the milk stains on their shoulders (incurred when burping is in progress), it is sensible to wear some sort of overall when the twins are being fed. It is possible to buy really pretty and practical cover ups suitable for this exercise.

QUESTIONS OF IDENTITY

To dress the twins alike or not, that is the question. The answer is to dress them alike if you want to while they are babes in arms and have no views on the subject, but to stop when they are old enough to differentiate between their clothes. Although not every mother would admit it, most of them experience reflected glory when people look at their two identically dressed babies and everyone's face breaks into a smile. Mothers of twins are justified in their pride and sense of achievement. Dressing them alike while they are tiny is a harmless pleasure which it would be silly to deny. Furthermore, there will certainly be many double presents of clothing and they might as well be put to good use.

However, as the twins get older, mothers should not make a fetish of their relationship. It becomes increasingly important to stress their differences rather than their similarities, in order to develop each one's individuality. Clothes can play a big role in this. If the twins are a boy and a girl, it is logical anyway to progress to different clothes for each. If they are unalike in colouring or other respects, what will suit one may not suit the other. Nor is it necessary to dress them totally differently. They can wear the same style of pullover, but the fact that one is blue and the other red is enough to give each a chance to develop not only his own awareness of himself but the knowledge that he is seen as a person in his own right.

Another very important reason for not dressing twins alike once they come into social contact with others, at playgroup or school, is to avoid confusion about who is who. One identical twin, long since grown up, remembers how she and her sister were irritated hundreds of times when people smiled at them and said, 'And now, which is which?' 'After all, we were not a party trick,' she says.

Even when not dressed the same, identical twins can easily be mistaken for each other, since they are not always together for comparisons to be made. The wise mother should see that some genuine or artificially created distinction is pointed out to visiting relatives or friends, other children or teachers. It could be a different hairstyle. In one set of identical girls, the mother had the bright idea of giving Rachel, the only one with an 'R' in her name a fRinge. Identical though they were, nobody who knew their names ever confused them.

An embroidered initial or a name somewhere on their clothes will also help to identify them individually. Hopefully, parents will have chosen names starting with different initials; while similar names can only add to the confusion: which is Ann-Mary and which Mary-Ann? Is that Christopher or Christian? If both twins have the same initial, they will curse their parents in later years when they open each other's letters by mistake.

Nobody should think that, having decided to dress the twins differently, that is the end of the matter. There is always Catch 22. Catch 22 means that when a mother comes home with one pale blue shirt and one dark blue, both twins will insist on having the dark blue. If one pair of trousers is embellished with four buttons and the other a decorative patch pocket, both children may be unyielding in their demands for the one, while the other will remain unworn unless you are prepared to quell the rebellion forcibly. The wily mother can usually find a way of upgrading the undesirable garment in the eyes of the unwilling recipient. It may be a question of adding something to it to change its appearance slightly or even a whispered communication that pale blue is really *her* favourite colour.

Not all children have strong views on what they wear, but as they get old enough to dress themselves it is good to let them get on with it. Twins are often much more self reliant, as well as more cooperative in helping each other to dress, than single children who may sit and wait for their mother to help. When they dress themselves, they may end up with a slightly bizarre costume: swimming pants and wellingtons may not be the best garb for the beginning of October nor will a delicate party dress be right for a session in the sandpit. Just as the way an adult dresses is an expression of his personality, the same applies to children and should be allowed within reason.

One twin spent a good three months attending playgroup wearing a different colour sock on each foot. He felt it made more sense than two socks of the same colour, and his mother saw no reason to get him to conform to normal sartorial usage. Another child would not be parted from a particular hat, known to him as his 'fireman's hat'. He wore it everywhere except in the bath and as often as not fell asleep with it askew on his head. At that age, eccentricity, if it can be called that, should be acceptable and what the neighbours think should not matter—if it ever does.

When the twins dress themselves, there may be times when they will don identical clothes on the same day, but this will probably happen because they both want to wear a certain garment and not because they have been conditioned to think of themselves as an indivisible unit. The choice is theirs and that is as it should be.

7 Articles Built for Two

Double this and double that
Oh how the money goes

Francis Day and Hunter

It is easy to pay out vast amounts of money on buying equipment for twins. It is also possible to spend comparatively little and still have all the essentials. Basically, the outlay depends not just on the number of items bought but on whether everything is new; some can be obtained second-hand, some may already be available because of an older child in the family, and other things may be given or lent.

Major items which are essential include cribs, cots, prams, pushchairs, baby chairs (otherwise called baby sitters), high chairs and a baby bath, although not all are needed at the beginning. Electric bottle-warmers and playpens are optional. Other requirements will be two potties, a nappy pail with lid, safety harnesses, a minimum of fourteen feeding bottles, a bottle brush, and a bucket or large bowl for sterilising bottles.

Unlike clothes buying, which has become easier over the years, obtaining hardware for twins presents difficulties. Nowhere is this more true than with prams. Pram manufacturers cater almost exclusively for the single child. Gone are the days of coachbuilt solidity, the Rolls Royce of the pram world—not perhaps the most fashionable but certainly the most sturdy baby carriage, able to stand up to the wear and tear inflicted not only by successive siblings but by successive generations.

PRAMS

Today's prams are all mass produced, either soft bodied or moulded steel. The majority have detachable bodies and collapsible wheel bases, enabling them to double as carrycots and to be carried in the boot of a car. Only half a dozen models are intended for twins—and this simply means they have some degree of extra stability and two hoods. Old-fashioned prams had wells for the occupants' legs when sitting; any isolated pram which has a well nowadays might accommodate the legs of a small doll but not a toddler's.

Twin prams are very costly but no wider or longer than single prams. They will, therefore, be suitable only for outings. For naps in the garden, they would soon defeat their purpose, since the two children would, after a few weeks, be unable to lie down full length and would kick each other awake.

When choosing a pram, certain factors should be borne in mind. The pram may weigh as much as 70lb. Add the weight of two six-month-old babies and you could find yourself stuck at the bottom of a hill, like one mother, who was quite unable to push them up again without the help of a passerby. Going downhill can actually be dangerous as the pram can run away with you. A light, soft-bodied model would be better if you live in a hilly area. Five-foot-nothing mothers should beware of buying high prams. Put the hood up before you decide on a model and make sure you can see over the top. Otherwise, on a wet day, you run the risk of collisions or a permanent crick in the neck from peering round the side. High prams have the advantages of carrying the babies at a height at which it is easier and more comfortable to attend to them, and out of reach of friendly dogs anxious to lick their faces. Their bigger wheels make roadside kerbs easier to negotiate, but smaller wheels are better and safer if the pram has to be manoeuvred up and down steps or stairs every day.

74

Before buying, check that the brakes are effective. They should lock two wheels securely and the brake lever should be so designed that a child cannot release it. Harness attachments must be safely anchored and there should be no fastenings on the apron which could be harmful if the babies tried to put them in their mouths. Hoods should collapse without pinching the mother's fingers, and pram bodies must incorporate a safety mechanism designed to make it impossible for them to collapse accidentally or to come off the wheel base unintentionally. Wheels should lock in place and replacements should be available in case of damage.

Prams are rarely as stable as they should be and manufacturers do not, on the whole, design them so that shopping can be carried home in them. Shopping trays resting on the wheel base are the only safe containers which will not upset the balance of the pram. Rightly or wrongly, the onus is put on the pram pusher to ensure that the occupants are safe. One manufacturer even goes so far as to attach a label to every pram which reads: 'The person in charge bears responsibility for the correct use and maintenance of this pram and the safety of the occupant. For full benefit from the safety requirements, it is essential that the child wears a British Standard safety belt properly fitted. Do not make the pram unstable with additional children or goods.'

Manufacturers appear to shrug off the fact that mothers with several young children may have no option about putting an additional child into a pram—particularly, of course, a single pram.

Twin prams have to be ordered several months in advance —long before most people know that they are going to have twins. If there is a history of twins in the family or any suspicion that an extra baby may be born, it is better to play safe. One big department store at least is happy to order a twin pram and, if it turns out that only a single is needed, will substitute another pram without any trouble. Because new prams are by no means necessarily better than old ones, the possibility of getting hold of a second-hand one should be considered. A used twin pram in good condition may provide better accommodation at a lower price. A really good single pram can be converted for twin use with extra stabilisation, a second hood and a different apron. The most beautiful single prams can sometimes be picked up for a song at jumble sales or through classified newspaper advertisements; it pays to keep your eyes open for these or perhaps to insert a 'want ad' yourself. Triplets are not catered for at all. The best thing to do is to get hold of the biggest, widest pram and put two at one end and one at the other.

Because the usefulness of a twin pram is fairly limited and the cost of a new one can be very high, a mother may decide to do without it altogether. Instead she can keep two single prams for garden use and invest in a good twin push-chair. Some of these pushchairs have fully adjustable foot and back rests, which are essential if they are used before the babies can sit up. For twins at a later stage, there are two basic versions: for two sitting side by side and for one sitting behind the other. The latter is to be recommended for fighters and hairpullers, as well as for people with very narrow doorways. Hairpullers in twin prams, incidentally, should wear mittens to protect the innocent.

When buying a twin pushchair, the same considerations apply as in choosing a pram with the extra proviso that a pushchair should fold easily for use when travelling by car, bus or train. Some models weigh as little as 11lb, others as much as 35lb, which can make a great deal of difference if they have to be carried. Most come with optional hoods and aprons, and one model has its own shopping tray underneath the seats.

The lightweight twin buggy is also available for three children. It has a width of 38 inches, which means that it will not pass through a standard door except sideways but it is better than nothing.

Families who produce a second set of twins before the first lot can walk are, of course, in trouble. Their choice is limited to finding the biggest pram possible and cramming four babies in like sardines; designing and building an alternative themselves; two people going out with two prams, or everyone staying at home. No toddler's seats exist to fit twin prams nor twin seats to fit single prams.

CRIBS AND COTS

The twins' first cribs can be carrycots, pram bodies, moses baskets, or cradles, from the most basic wicker or plastic-covered cardboard to the most glorious creation complete with flounces, frills and canopy. If money is tight, it may not be worth investing a great deal of money for an item to be dispensed with after about four months. A few yards of shirred gingham or curtain netting fastened around an old crib will transform the most utilitarian object into a thing of beauty.

As the twins outgrow their first cribs, the normal follow-on will be 4ft by 2ft drop-side cots, which will last until the children are about four. Some of these cots have two positions for the mattress: a high one for minimum bending over newborn infants and a low one to discourage toddlers climbing out. The really determined explorer is still going to climb out sooner or later. If that is the case, it may be advisable to leave the drop side permanently down, rather than risk accidents. One mother remembers the time when her two-year-old tearabouts played a nightly game of daring-do, balancing on the cot rail and roaring with laughter as she ran from one cot to the other, giving each one a gentle shove back again. Eventually one twin made it and the result was a broken arm.

Second-hand cots are easy to come by. After all, what use are they once they are outgrown? Giving it a coat of paint (non-lead, of course) or just stripping the old paint and varnishing, and putting in a new mattress will make one as good as new. If the metal rods fastening the cot side are bent, replacements are available from shops.

When the kids have outgrown their cots, bunks may seem the best solution, if there is a space problem. However, think twice if yours are boisterous children, particularly if they are given to fighting. If bunk beds are bought, there may be constant squabbling over who sleeps on top. Bunks have side rails to prevent a child accidentally falling out, but that is not to say that one cannot push the other out. With small thugs (and that's most little boys), parents who value their peace of mind may prefer to instal the space-saving beds which slide under each other during the day or which fold up into the wall when not in use. Where there is no shortage of space, two normal beds would be the best buy.

PRACTICAL AIDS

A place set aside for changing and dressing the babies makes life easier. Continental mothers have a *Wickelkommode*, a waist-high, wide chest of drawers with a railing around three sides and a terry-covered mattress on top of it. The drawers hold clothes and nappies; and the top makes a safe and practical surface for attending to the baby. Any chest of the right dimensions can be converted along these lines (apart from the railing) by padding the top with a pretty towelling or plastic cloth-covered blanket and securing them firmly. A ready-made alternative is the baby dresser and storage unit made by Mothercare. A padded changing mat makes an easily cleaned surface for nappy changing, plus providing pockets for cotton wool, pins and lotions.

Not the right way to change two at once!

Although not essential, electric bottle warmers are very useful, enabling bottles to be warmed up not only at night but during the day while the babies are being changed prior to feeding, without the mother having to leave the room. It is a false economy to buy only one, in which case the two bottles will never be at the right temperature at the same time. But a word of warning: bacteria will thrive if milk is left just keeping warm.

Low baby chairs, sometimes called baby sitters, are particularly useful with twins. They make for easy bottle and spoon feeding, as well as enabling the mother to take a wakeful baby from room to room while she gets on with other duties. Some have stands to convert them into high chairs, others can be slung from chairs or used in cars. When the babies become more active, sturdier high chairs take over. Proper safety harnesses are needed for these chairs, as well as with prams and pushchairs, of course.

Baby baths come in various shapes and sizes. Some have a sloping back to support the baby, some an outlet hose which is safer and easier if the bathwater has to be emptied in a downstairs bathroom. Some are rigid, others fold up for easy storage.

PLAYPENS

Few parents have found playpens a worthwhile investment for twins. Many children hate them and scream from the moment they are put into one. Some twins bang each other over the head with toys and have to be given a playpen each, leaving little extra space in a room. Few children tolerate such a curtailment of their personal liberty for more than a few weeks anyway. It is often better to borrow or hire a pen for the short duration of its usefulness.

An alternative adopted by many parents is to cordon off part of a room or a hallway, giving the children greater freedom while still keeping them safe. One mother who cordoned of part of her hall, securely fastened a stairgate across the open front door in summer, so that her children could watch the comings and goings in the street which they found highly entertaining. Extendable trellis is useful for fencing off a small area indoors, and will also make the garden safe for toddlers, keeping them away from potentially dangerous steps, for instance; but it must be securely fixed so that small fingers cannot be caught. With a barrier, the children can stay in the garden safely without constant supervision.

8 One Pair of Hands

The mother's problem with twins in the household is not really to find the time to see to their daily needs but to accommodate all the other things which need doing, like the cooking, housework, laundry and shopping. Before giving any thought to the ways and means in which these chores can be tackled most easily, the mother must get her priorities straight and decide what is important and what is not.

Twins do initially involve more work than single children and it is necessary to organise the day in such a way that the household essentials get done and the unnecessary chores are postponed until later or consciously abandoned for a year or two—by that time, they may not need doing at all! Some people deal with correspondence very successfully in this way; they find that, if they leave it long enough, some letters no longer require an answer! Work can be eliminated by thinking ahead. One mother of twins went around her house with a large cardboard box into which she placed all the useless little knicknacks which just collected dust. They all went into the cellar—together with the two tucked and pleated baby outfits, which had four minute buttons at each cuff and six at the neck; worn once, they had to be hand washed and took half an hour each to iron.

CUTTING CORNERS

Housework needs rationalising. It is neither pleasant nor advisable to live in a pigsty, but a little common sense will soon show where work is needed and where energy can be conserved. The nursery must be kept clean and the floor washed regularly and this will become more important as the twins spend more time crawling on it. The same applies

81

to the kitchen where food preparation requires hygienic conditions and where the children will also be spending time. However, floor polishing, while good for the floor and perhaps satisfying to the eyes, is not necessary, and the same goes for polishing furniture and dusting.

The laundry has to be done—and done very frequently. What starts off as a small pile of dirty linen grows into a large mountain of laundry, as the kids need bigger clothes, crawl all over the place and make mud pies. So, however tight money may be, it is not an economy to save on laundry aids. The more automatic the washing machine, the less time needs to be spent supervising its operations. A fully automatic machine can be switched on at midnight and left to cope unaided, disgorging clean washing the next morning, ready to hang up.

Spin driers speed drying enormously and most mothers feel that if it is a question of buying either a washing machine or a spin drier, then the second is a better purchase. Nothing is more depressing than rooms festooned with strings of damp nappies and nothing smells worse than steaming woollies in front of a fire. If fond grandparents chip in, then get a tumble drier as well because, apart from the certainty of having clean dry clothes when they are needed, it obviates the need to hang up wet laundry and take it down when it is dry—not forgetting the extra times this has to be done when it starts to rain. It also takes the wrinkles out of most clothes, leaving an even smaller pile for ironing.

If your husband is a three-piece-suit man, who would not dream of being caught in his shirt sleeves, you need only iron the bits of his shirt that show. Men's shirts take ages to fold and it is much quicker and more sensible to hang them up unfolded. Buy and use easy-care fabrics wherever possible and forget about ironing bed linen, kitchen towels and underwear. Learn to fold an unironed sheet neatly before putting it on top of the pile. If a fresh sheet is always taken from the bottom, by the time the folded one has got there, it will be beautifully pressed. After one night's use, it will be totally indistinguishable from an ironed one. If there is any ironing left to do, sit down to it; it's more restful.

SHOPPING AND STORING

All good organisation involves planning ahead and infrequent big shopping expeditions save time, money and nerves. Plan to shop when it is most convenient—not when the bread and toilet paper have run out and there is no more washing powder. Keep a pad hanging in the kitchen and make a note when the flour is running low, or you are getting to the end of the baby lotion, or it's Aunt Sarah's birthday in a fortnight and you have to get her a card.

With a family that has certainly grown to four and may well number more, the moment comes very soon when the previous normal quantities of shopping—like 3lb of potatoes, half a dozen eggs, one small loaf and 2lb of apples—shoot up to 5lb of this, two dozen of that and a case of the other. Take advantage of the one remaining greengrocer who delivers, even if he is not the one you normally patronise; remember that the milkman can usually bring a lot besides milk to the door, and investigate the possibilities of bulk buying.

Double quantities usually cost twice as much, although some reductions are normal when buying a packet of ten fishfingers instead of six or an economy-size tube of toothpaste instead of a small one. There is money to be saved when buying in quantity—and not only from the conventional discount houses and warehouses which advertise to this effect. A local grocer or chemist (not belonging to a chain) should give reductions on cases of baby food or tinned milk, and disposable nappies will cost less if bought in bulk.

Investment in a freezer will enable you to take advantage of food bargains and bulk buying. If space is limited, it can be housed in a garage or shed, provided electricity is laid on,

83

or in a cellar. Second-hand or reconditioned models can be bought, and even old ice-cream freezers and shop 'conservators' are perfectly adequate for frozen-food storage. Your freezer will not only help you to economise on shopping expeditions and the cost of food, but will permit cooking in bulk. Seven pounds of apples, cooked and then puréed, can be split into small portions for freezing and thawing out as needed—as opposed to doing the individual operations perhaps fourteen times over to get the same results.

Bulk buying can cause storage problems. Without turning the home into a warehouse, it may be possible to accommodate, say, 56lb of detergent under the stairs, cartons of tinned milk in a shed and packets of disposable nappies in a wardrobe or under a bed. If the quantities involved in bulk buying are much larger than is warranted for your own household, or involves a greater outlay of cash than is available in one lump, friends or neighbours may be keen to participate. There will be less to store, but the financial advantages and reduced shopping expeditions will be shared by all. One small family, together with four friends, decided to buy all their vegetables and fruit at the wholesale market. Every two or three weeks, a different family phoned around the other members to find out what produce they wanted and a rough shopping list was drawn up. A crate of apples, two boxes of oranges, a sack of carrots or potatoes and a few trays of strawberries are easily disposed of. By noting down prices paid and spending an hour at home weighing out everyone's share and totting up each bill, a real saving can be effected. The more people who participate in such joint purchasing ventures, the less frequently it is anyone's turn to go to market. If none of your friends wants to share, put up a notice at the local clinic or in a shop window, asking anyone interested in bulk buying to contact you.

If all else fails, enlist your husband's aid to do the bulky shopping or find someone who will sit with the twins while you do it. Shopping in quantity without a car and with babes in arms is awkward and time consuming. Supermarkets are only just beginning to realise that mothers are not prepared to leave infants unattended in their prams outside the store. Some chains have introduced trolleys which have an infant carrier as well as the now usual toddler seat. But, the economics of the business being what they are, nobody spares a thought for the mother of twins. Unless you are prepared to go into shops with the babies tied to you papoose-fashion—in which case you will cause such a stir that you will be unable to concentrate on finding the baked beans because of the procession behind you—it is better to

postpone shopping expeditions *à trois* for a while. Once the twins are able to sit up, it is possible to put one child in the body of the trolley and use a second trolley for your purchases. If everything and everybody are put in one trolley, apart from leaving very little room for what you buy, the kids will probably proceed to throw out or unwrap everything as soon as you have put it in.

TIME OFF

What about the needs of the mother around whom every-thing revolves? Having found her feet in the new role, she will no doubt feel that she has enough on her plate not to look around for any extra-mural activities. In the first few months at least, it is certainly better that she should not overextend herself. There comes a time quite soon, how-ever, when a nonstop domestic and maternal routine is not wholly satisfying for many people, even if there is enough to do to keep them busy. Many intelligent women need the extra stimulus of something quite unconnected with their daily life.

The mothers who cope well and are contented and happy are frequently those who continue to pursue some outside interest, to however limited an extent. Getting out of the house for an hour or two a week will help to relieve the sometimes humdrum existence of mothers of young children. Some have careers which can at a later stage be pursued on a part-time or occasional basis. The qualified teacher or nurse should have no difficulty in getting one session of work to suit herself, providing she can find someone to replace her in the home. Anyone desperate to get out occasionally, but with no obvious mother substitute available, should try to team up with another mother to take turns in looking after both lots of children. An extra couple of children will be little or no more trouble to look after than your own, and the knowledge that the reciprocal arrange-ment will give you some regular time to call your own is invaluable. A few hours to yourself, removed from the scene of your daily activity, will make you a better mother the rest of the time.

Nor is it necessary to stop all social life because the family has multiplied. It may not be the moment for your husband to invite his boss to dinner, but friends are friends and do not stand on ceremony. One mother took the opportunity to hand her visitors a hungry baby to feed at 10 pm. Another continued to play music with a group of friends, sometimes with a baby on her knees. In short, the more you put into life, the more you get out of it. It is up to the individual to arrange her life so as to create the opportunity of doing something she wants to do.

HELP IN THE HOUSE

Grandmothers, who in today's small family unit society are all too often sad and solitary, virtually cut off from their married children, used to play a valuable role in extended family life, not only helping to ease the burden on the young mother but performing a useful task and thereby retaining their self respect and a justified feeling of being needed. In the Mediterranean countries and other parts of the world, the grandmother is still very much in evidence. Cypriot mothers, to whom I have talked, all enjoy the physical and moral support of having someone in the family who knows the ropes. For the vast majority of women, however, coming home with their babies means coping alone, unless they have the means to pay for help in the house.

Help can be a boon with twins. However, the advice most frequently handed out, to get help even if it means going into the red, is, to my mind, not very practical. Sleepless nights spent worrying about an ever-increasing deficit in the family budget will add to the problems rather than relieve them. If there is enough money to spare, then it is a good idea to decide where paid help would be most valuable.

If there is an extra room available, the most generally sought-after help is the au pair. In return for free board and lodging and a fair sum of pocket money, she should, in theory, spend half of every weekday working for you. If you have space but not the money, a partial solution could be to let the room at a reduced or non-existent rent to a student, in exchange for a given number of hours' help. Others, with some money but no room, may find that paying someone to clean for a few hours is the most useful plan.

Local welfare services do not provide help to mothers of twins unless they feel it to be particularly necessary. Nevertheless, the health visitor is the person through whom any requests for council help should be channelled. If she considers it necessary, she can arrange for a home help to be sent. According to the family finances, home helps may be provided free or at a nominal rate. In case of need and in conjunction with the Women's Royal Voluntary Service, the health visitor can arrange for prams and clothes or bedding to be provided for the babies. She will also, incidentally, arrange for domiciliary family planning if the mother cannot get out to a family planning clinic.

However enviable the thought of an extra pair of hands may be, in practice not every helper is worth having. One mother who was offered a hospital nurse for a couple of hours a day by her local council was indeed fortunate. But the nurse considered her duty was only to help with the feeding. Whatever time she arrived—and it varied—she grabbed the bottles, grabbed the babies, fed them, burped them and shot out again, leaving them quite unsettled by this rush, rush, rush routine. Another received a few hours nursing help from her enlightened council but when the helper repeatedly and pointedly said, 'We can't have daddy coming through the nursery, can we?' the mother decided she would rather manage on her own.

Au pairs, so potential employers are always told, will look after children and do a little light housework. Not infrequently, the situation arises where the au pair takes the kids out to the park, while the mother stays at home to scrub the floors! So, before rushing out and getting help, it is as well to establish where it is most needed and where the least conflict is likely to arise. As any employer of au pairs or other help will tell you, the wrong person is not only highly unsettling for the whole family but far worse than no help at all.

The girl who cannot wash up without breaking something or the one who spends an hour in the bathroom at rush hour are dubious assets, while anyone who cannot be trusted with the children is better dispensed with immediately.

Without exception, the best workers are those who arrive and simply get on with what needs doing in the home: the schoolgirl, sent by the council's Good Neighbour service, who went straight to the kitchen sink full of dirty dishes; the home help who changed the bed linen and made the beds; the cleaning lady who whipped round the house, creating order out of chaos, and the au pair who, having finished one task turned up to ask, 'What shall I do now?' instead of retiring to her room. All were remembered with affection by mothers and proved to be worth their weight in gold.

On the other hand, the girl who ate all the ice cream and put cat food on the children's sandwiches; the one who always overslept; the cleaner who managed to hoover away all the children's toys together with the dust, and the girl who allowed the toddlers to go on a high slide in the park after having been forbidden to do so were all duds whose help was not worth having.

Looking back on four years of coping with twins, one young mother said that during the first year what she really needed was not conventional help but a cooked meal 'because I did not have the energy to do any cooking myself'. 'Meals on wheels' are not for able-bodied mothers, no matter how many children they have. Yet a neighbour, who cooks for her family anyway, might be prepared and happy to add an extra helping to her saucepans for such a mother; or food could be brought to the house ready for heating up whenever the mother has time to eat it.

Another mother mentioned the mending which just never got done. Shirts without collar buttons, socks with holes, sheets with tears which will get larger need to be tackled at some point. An advertisement on a card in a shop window might catch the attention of an old age pensioner or someone glad to earn a little money by taking home the mending.

Housewives do not normally hire anyone to do the shopping, but getting to the shops can sometimes, if not always, become a major enterprise, depending on the number of

children to be got ready, and may prove impossible if one of them is ill. It could be a tremendous help to find someone able to shop on one's behalf or to sit with the children while the mother goes out on her own to buy what she needs.

The moral of the story is to know yourself and thereby to know what chores to pass on to someone else. Whether or not you ask the health visitor for help, good neighbours exist well outside any social services scheme and some problems can be solved very easily by coming to an arrangement with a neighbour. For instance, your husband takes the neighbour's child and your elder child to playgroup in the morning, and she brings both back at lunchtime, when you are busy with the twins.

As time goes on, the twins themselves will be helpful to the mother and to each other. They are often more understanding than the single child would be of the extra burden on their mother's shoulders. One little girl was overheard telling her friend, 'Mummy can't really cope, you know. She has two sets of twins.' Twins are good at helping each other and respond with pleasure to requests such as, 'Paul, will you help Christopher with his shoes,' or 'Mary, can you wash Jonathan's face please.'

Single children are inevitably separated by age, and mothers often expect the eldest to be more responsible or helpful. But twins frequently develop an equal responsibility for each other. As they grow older, twins in the family entail no more work, and sometimes less, than two children of different ages. Indeed there are advantages of having two at the same stage of development and with the same interests, instead of finding—as often happens—that what is fun for a younger child is boring for the elder. Twins have the advantage of a ready-made playmate of the same age, a sharer of secrets and an ally in adversity, someone whose presence prevents loneliness and boredom.

9 The Twins' Progress

O'er the rugged mountain brow
Clara threw the twins she nursed
And remarked 'I wonder now
Which will reach the bottom first.'

Harry Graham

At birth, most twins are lighter and smaller than singles. They may be as much as 3in shorter but, by the age of five, the difference will only be about 1in. Although the final adult height is more likely to be influenced by genetic make up, so that the children of tall parents will themselves be tall, the most frequently cited statistics, taken from a study of Swedish army recruits, showed that twins were on average $\frac{1}{2}$in shorter.

When comparisons are made between the weights and heights of other children and the twins, the mother must not necessarily expect them to be equal. Even singles cannot be compared in this respect with each other, any more than adults, except out of curiosity. A weekly weigh-in in the first few months is a good idea, but all any mother needs to know is whether the individual child is doing well.

HEALTH

Inexperienced mothers, particularly those with newly arrived twins, are the ones most likely to want to seek confirmation that their babies are thriving. The local infant welfare clinics and the health visitor are there to help. The clinics are designed to keep tabs on a child's physical progress, to advise mothers on feeding and other problems, to provide medical check-ups, and to give the inoculations and vaccinations necessary to protect the baby from some of the more serious illnesses. Infant welfare clinics are for healthy babies and they do an excellent job. This free service is particularly welcome when one considers what conscientious mothers in countries without such medical welfare arrangements have to pay to pediatricians for similar advice and protection.

However, mothers of twins often find themselves unable to take advantage of these facilities because quite a few clinics simply do not consider their practical needs. Any clinic situated at the top of a flight of stairs is going to be difficult to visit. Frequently there is just one cot, already occupied by another baby, so that the mother has nowhere to deposit the first twin while she goes down to get the second. Since mothers do not like leaving their babies unattended in a pram in the street, such a clinic is a non-starter for mothers of twins. Even if the clinic is purpose-built and has ramps allowing the pram to be wheeled in, if the main purpose of the visit is the weekly weigh-in, the twin mother is likely to change her mind soon enough about attending. The normal drill is to undress the baby, wait for his turn to be weighed, place the resentful bundle on the cold scales, which are usually covered only with a sheet of tissue paper, and then dress him. Try doing this with twins—weighing first one, then the other and finally dressing two on your lap simultaneously. It is infinitely more sensible and agreeable to hire or borrow a pair of baby scales and do it at home, where they can be weighed before bath time in ten trouble-free seconds.

Medical check-ups, are, of course, very necessary to ensure that all is well and this is particularly important for twins with very low birth-weights, who are more vulnerable to audio, visual and locomotory problems. The health visitor is likely to make a special effort to ensure regular clinic attendance of such small babies but, if the family doctor runs a baby clinic too, this may be preferable.

The doctor may even be willing to visit the twins at home

for check-ups, just as he would if they were ill and the mother unable to bring them to see him. The health visitor will call on you in any case. She normally comes on the eleventh day after the birth but, should the twins have to stay in hospital longer, it would be a little later. Provided she and the mother hit it off together, the health visitor can be a valuable friend and adviser with whom to discuss problems and general progress. If requested, she will do her best to come regularly, knowing how difficult it can be for the mother to get to the clinic.

There are exceptions to every rule and the health visitor who rubs you up the wrong way is better dispensed with. One mother reports her health visitor's cries of horror when she discovered the twins were being fed on manufactured baby foods. 'Home cooking is so much better,' she said to the mother, who had no help and could not remember when she last had a cooked meal herself. 'Cooee, I'm here,' announced another, as she tripped in and settled herself comfortably in the kitchen. 'I do love dropping in on you at coffee time and watching you busy yourself with your twins.' And a third, who muttered darkly and inaudibly about egg yolks and apple and beans, left countless mothers confused and worried about the order in which they should introduce various solids into their infants' diets.

The sensible mother will take what is good and reject what is bad. A good clinic and health visitor are invaluable. The birth of new babies frequently coincides with a move to a different neighbourhood and the clinic automatically brings a mother into contact with other young mothers. For those who are too shy to make such contact themselves, the health visitor may be able to put one mother in touch with another who lives nearby.

Children can now be immunised against a number of illnesses which would be dangerous or fatal if caught at an early age or if caught at all. It is very important, therefore, to visit the clinic or doctor's surgery when inoculations are due.

With twins, it is advisable to keep a record of the injections each child has had and when. It is by no means unknown for one child to be given the same inoculation twice and for his twin to remain unprotected because of a mix-up. This is particularly likely to happen if, for some reason, the twins are not inoculated at the same time. Of course, doctors and clinics keep records for every patient, but the mother herself may make a mistake if she sometimes goes to the clinic and sometimes to the doctor. If in doubt, the local Medical Officer of Health's department keeps records regarding immunisation which can be checked.

It is essential for mothers of twins to keep a notebook in which not only vaccinations and inoculations are entered for each child but also the occurrence of infectious diseases. What may appear likely to leave an indelible memory when it is all happening will quickly recede as other events take their place, and it can be of the utmost importance in later life to know whether either or both twins had mumps or German measles and which twin had an anti-tetanus jab after he cut his foot. Write it down when it happens and keep the book in a safe place.

If one of the babies appears to be ill, the doctor will, of course, be consulted. What if the other one remains as fit as a fiddle? Should they be kept together or separated? Obviously, medical opinion decides, but if it is a question of colds, flu and all the usual minor childhood illnesses you do not separate them unless the other twin is delicate and has to be specially protected. In general, both children are very likely to catch the same illnesses anyway and it is very much easier for the mother if they both have them at the same time instead of one falling ill just as the other is recovering.

With some of the common childhood illnesses, it is a positive advantage for children—but not babies—to catch them, rather than wait until adult life when they can produce harmful complications. There has been quite a vogue for

German measles parties, for instance, designed to produce immunity to that disease which is dangerous to the unborn child when contracted by a pregnant woman. It is also better for boys to catch mumps before puberty, as it can affect the fertility of adult males.

Experiences vary regarding whether twins wake each other when an ailing one is fretful but, on the whole, it appears to be rare and there should not be any need to put them in separate rooms just to ensure unbroken sleep. A dimmer-switch for the nursery light or a low wattage lamp at night-time will enable you to see what you are doing without waking the twin who is asleep and should remain so. A divan in the babies' room can cut down on parents' nocturnal journeys when there is an unhappy patient to be comforted.

If one of the children should become really ill and has to go into hospital or be isolated, some care must be taken to prevent the separation of the twins having a harmful effect. With identical twins especially, the absence of the best-loved being of all can be very distressing. In a wartime study of identical twins in a residential nursery, Mrs Dorothy Burlingham noted that twins reacted to separation from each other in a way similar to the toddler parted from its mother. They expressed loneliness, withdrew from company, wished to be alone and collected presents for the absent one. Some insisted on being dressed in their twin's clothes or only responded when addressed by the absent twin's name.

Mrs Burlingham also discovered that such children in mourning—which they were—were comforted by their own mirror image since they recognised in it not themselves—small children do not often see their own reflection—but their identical twin, with whose features they were familiar. Thus Jessie looked at herself in the mirror and smilingly said 'My Bessie'. When it was possible for the healthy twin to visit the sickroom, however briefly, it gave reassurance and comfort.

DEVELOPMENT

Regarding the normal physical development of twins, there are no rules about who does what first. One study seems to indicate that the heavier twin tends to be dominant and marginally more intelligent; certainly low birth-weight frequently has a delaying effect on development. Where both weights are very low, the twin with the lower weight has even farther to catch up. Another theory postulates that identical twins have an alternating pattern of development, so that one may sit up first, the second stand first, the first walk before the second, and so on. Girls are usually quicker off the mark than boys. Although one twin may appear dominant, it is sometimes found that the apparently passive one in fact asserts himself just as much.

In developing a baby's mind, one of the most important aids is the stimulus of the mother's conversation—not the conversation which goes on around him but that which is directed towards him. The more time the mother spends talking to the child, the greater his verbal development and ability to absorb more new information and to build on his knowledge.

When it comes to assessing intelligence, there is evidence that twins, for a while, do less well than single children, if verbal factors play a role in the assessment. One of the likely reasons for this is that twins perforce have less individual maternal attention.

Recent research shows that mothers spend the same amount of time per day with twins as they do with single children. So, twins can be said to get only half the exclusive face-to-face contact with their mothers that single children have; this has an effect on their verbal development. Statistics show that pre-school language development among twins is between three to six months' delayed. By the time they are eleven years old, IQ tests, in which language is a factor, show that twins score on average two to three points lower than singles.

Another possible reason for this delay, which is only temporary, is the twins' smaller birth-weight, but the reduced verbal contact is thought to be a big factor, not compensated for by any private language developed between them. In the case of one surviving twin, his IQ was found to be nearly the same as that of the single child. This phenomenon of delayed speech development is not, however, unique to twins. In large families, where children have less contact with adults and are more frequently left to play with each other, there is also a lower IQ rating where verbal competence is a factor.

Although most parents of twins are aware of and sometimes concerned by the fact that they cannot often devote undivided attention to each child, and although mothers do not by magic find extra hours in the day in which to look after their twins, the knowledge that spending time with each one is invaluable may nevertheless help them to provide it. That is not to say that a mother would want to create any artificial schoolroom atmosphere, but simply to be a responsive, communicative parent, aware of each child's individual needs. Nor should a mother tear herself in half in the effort, and feel guilty every time the twins are treated as a unit; it is unavoidable that this should happen. The chatty mother will augment her children's vocabulary anyway, without even trying.

10 Alone and Together

We do everything alike
We look alike, we dress alike, we talk alike
and what is more we hate each other very much.

sung by Danny Kaye
(© 1937, 1953 De Sylva, Brown & Henderson Inc)

How does twinhood manifest itself, do twins have a special relationship, is there a private language in which they communicate, do they like the same things, do they share, have they got the same tastes, are they telepathic, do they both fall ill at the same time, are they both good at the same things, do they stick up for each other? These are questions asked by people who are captivated and fascinated by the twins they see or read about.

Identical twins, though looking alike, may have very different characters, abilities and habits from one another; but, having the same genes and chromosomes, there is every likelihood that they will have more pronounced similarities than fraternal twins. Fraternals are no more alike genetically than any two siblings, although they will presumably share the same environment and be exposed to the same stimuli to a far greater extent than would be possible for differently aged brothers or sisters.

A SPECIAL RELATIONSHIP

Certainly the implicit and unspoken understanding that some twins enjoy tends to be confined to identicals. The physical presence of the other is very important while they are growing up, and attempts at any real separation often misfire. What bothers the one can trouble the other, what one dreams of having, the other wants too.

99

The need for togetherness can obviously start before birth. When Joanna and Geraldine were born, one had to go into an incubator for a couple of days; the other refused the breast until the moment her twin returned. Mothers with babes in arms mention that if one twin is taken out of the room, the other becomes fretful. One mother says that when one small baby dirties his nappies without crying, the other one, although clean herself, will begin wailing within a few minutes. When Timothy and John were transferred into big cots, they became very fretful and only settled down again when their mother realised that they could not see each other from their cots; after they had been moved into a different position, all was well.

Real absence from each other can have unforseen consequences. When two twelve-year-olds heard they were each to spend a term at a school in France in order to improve their French, they were quite excited at the prospect and the first one went off quite happily. The one who stayed at home was also quite contented but, on the day her sister left, she developed a cold which remained for three months until her twin returned. And the same thing happened when the second one left.

When Hugh broke his leg in a tobogganing accident and went into hospital, his twin, David, pined to such an extent that, within a fairly short period, what started as a cold became so much worse that he also had to be hospitalised.

When it comes to language, some twins certainly do develop their own. It seems only natural, however, and not a mystical occurrence, that two babies brought up side by side should develop a method of communication which makes sense to them if not necessarily to others. Parents of single children can usually interpret the garbled pidgin English used by their offspring. While doting aunts and fond grandparents look on uncomprehendingly, the mother interprets the baby's special words for bottle, blanket, dog or whatever. She knows their meaning because the baby's most constant contact is with her and so she understands his language better than anyone else, particularly as he is aping her words. Twins, however, normally spend twenty-four hours out of every day in each other's company and their attempts at communication are perforce mainly directed towards each other and not to the mother, and since they do not have an adult vocabulary their sounds can be very difficult to interpret. In the language of twins, the mother is a comparative outsider, the foreigner who cannot understand the lingo!

Some twins continue to use their private language when they are older, not as a substitute for English or whatever language they speak, but as a secret means of communication at school, for instance, only understood by each other. Plenty of children evolve and adopt secret languages, readily understood by the initiated but mumbo jumbo to adults. The only difference is that one has its spontaneous origins in infancy and does not use normal language construction and the other is based on a code.

Twins often call each other by nicknames—Haji and Baji, Ama and Lolo are examples—but these are less likely to be the result of any special relationship than of a toddler's inability to pronounce complicated syllables. Parents are much to blame for perpetuating their children's baby talk—because they love to listen to it. What starts as a baby's attempt to get his mouth round an awkward name, ends up as a permanent nickname. 'Poopoo' may be cute for eighteen-month-old Pauline, but not so hot when she brings her boy friend home for the first time and the family refers to her as such!

Because some twins do seem to think alike, the situation can arise when other people seem to be hearing an echo. The schoolteacher of an identical pair took one of them to task in the playground for asking a question to which she had given a detailed answer ten minutes before in the classroom. She was surprised when told that the other question must have come from his twin (who was in a parallel class) because both the content of the question and the words used were the same. Many parents comment on the frequency with which twins will say the same thing virtually at the same time, without any collusion.

John's family have mentioned that, although his twin brother, Billy, has led a separate existence for many years, when he comes back for a visit, it has happened more than once that both have burst into song spontaneously, singing the same phrase of music. John says that his wife has been astonished on a couple of occasions when he has answered the telephone and said 'Hallo Billy.' On neither occasion did John even think about the fact that he was greeting his twin, who at the time was living abroad and with whom he did not even get on particularly well; he just knew instinctively that it was Billy calling.

When the same thing happens to twins independently, almost at the same time, is it coincidence? Or is it some special condition of twinhood? Do they have the same impulses at the same time or what? Some happenings are more easily rationalised than others. When one toddler woke up to go to the bathroom during the night, he was inevitably followed by his twin who arrived within seconds. Here one could conclude that it was not so much a similar physiological make-up, but a heightened and almost sub-conscious awareness of each other which made them both wake up at the same time for the same reason.

Twins who set out independently to buy each other a birthday card and present and come back with identical cards and gifts are very much in tune with each other and not uncommon. However, husbands and wives also sometimes buy each other the same present. Twin middle-aged lawyers, when asked whether they had ever bought each other the same birthday present, replied with one voice, 'But we never buy each other presents.' They really did illustrate an exceptionally close bond by going on to explain, 'It would be like buying a present for oneself.'

Telepathy or extra-sensory perception are perhaps sometimes no more than an awareness of another familiar person's thought processes heightened to a greater extent than is usual. Husbands and wives frequently have the same impulses at the same time, or some prior knowledge of what the other is about to do. Parents, too, are sometimes more than intuitive of what goes on in their children's minds. After all, people do quite frequently say of another person, 'I can read her thoughts like a book.' One eighteen-year-old never failed to be amazed—and annoyed—that she could only rarely take her mother by surprise by appearing without warning on her doorstep. One lived in London, the other in the country. Visits were not all that frequent, but premonitions often preceded them.

The phenomenon of identical twins needing glasses with the same optical prescription or having exactly similar temperature charts when both are ill is perhaps understandable. But when two sixty-year-old brothers both injure their Achilles tendon in the same week, although one lives in England and the other in Australia, the explanation is more elusive. What of the two brothers who each had an identical car accident on the same stretch of road on the same night but in different cars? Then there is the experience of the family on holiday who went swimming; one identical twin cut his foot on the bottom of the pool and the mother took him to the first aid station. Returning from there, she met her husband with the other twin who had cut his foot in the same place. The other three children did not cut their feet.

The type of experience often associated with twins happened to Jonathan, newly married and living in London. Normally a very healthy individual, he developed a sudden agonising pain in his side, which made his wife wonder whether she should get him to hospital quickly. An hour and a half later, a friend telephoned from Wales to say that Jonathan's twin brother had just been taken to hospital there for an emergency appendicitis operation. Jonathan's pain left him forthwith.

On the cerebral plane there is the tale of two identicals who passed the same eight and failed the same two 'O' levels. In a scholarship examination entered by 300 children they came within four places of each other, and, in a later university entrance exam, both twins not only tackled the same questions, but discovered afterwards that in one question they had both decided to reject the obvious argument— which they assumed the other would use—in favour of a more devious one. And, of course, they both did the same thing. Other twins report always tying for place in exams, but there are plenty more who never have the same results.

All such similarities of thought and experience tend to relate only to identical twins, although it is surprising how frequently fraternal twins, particularly while they are small, are found sleeping in the same position. Thumb-sucking baby twins have also been known to lie side by side, eyes firmly shut, happily sucking each other's thumb!

Being a twin can have enormous advantages. Most echo the sentiments of one six-year-old who said, 'It's not much fun at school when Markie is at home with a cold. After all, he is my best friend.' A twin is often a best friend for life, someone who is more in tune with one's thoughts than anyone else and, while they are small, someone who makes strange new situations less daunting. Little twins cannot always visualise life without one another. 'Who will our wife be when we grow up?' asked one three-year-old.

'I'm going to marry Chris,' said another of her twin brother, 'and we will adopt our children.'

Not all twins are happy in their relationship though. They may grow up in a state of constant warfare, and some start early. Still at the baby stage, one little girl would take her brother's bottle away, drink his milk and return his bottle empty without the parents being any the wiser for some time.

Some parents complain sadly that their twins seem to spend all their time fighting with each other. A few twins, more often fraternal, give the impression of having exhausted the possibilities of a friendly relationship with each other while still in the womb! They are not necessarily competitive, but are either not interested in each other or downright hostile. It is best not to push such relationships, to treat each one as an individual and not be surprised if they do not have the same wishes or reactions. Fraternal twins are often as different as chalk and cheese, and quite a few parents comment on the fact that no one would ever guess they were twins. Differences in build, temperament, ability and personality are all good reasons for not expecting similarities in other respects. Such twins sometimes only begin to enjoy each other's company after they have grown up and live apart.

Whatever sentimental ideas parents may have about the joys of brotherhood and sisterhood, and the happy united family group they would like to form, wishful thinking is not going to change the relationship from one of irritation or indifference or comparative tolerance to one of great friendship. Better by far to accept it and let each twin develop in his own way. They are, after all, two separate human beings who, though they may have certain features or characteristics in common, still have distinct identities.

Unlike single children, twins come into the world at the same time and, in the normal way, are brought up in the same manner by the same parents. They never enjoy the advantage of being the only baby, and must share virtually everything and everybody with each other from the beginning. Some twins share quite happily, most of them accepting the principle of sharing with outsiders rather more easily than single children who have not had to do so previously. But sharing their mother's affection is often a more difficult concept. Mothers of twins have to develop particularly accommodating and spacious laps, as the arrival of one twin on her lap is usually followed immediately by the second.

The mother's aim is to give her offspring a happy childhood which will, at the same time, prepare them to take their place in society as well-adjusted adults, able to pursue happy and useful lives. By recognising that each twin is capable of thinking, acting and behaving as a complete individual, they will be equipped eventually to stand on their own two feet.

Common sense will, therefore, decree that, at a stage and age where the children become aware of wanting them, they are given individual possessions and clothes. They must also know that in their parents' eyes each one is unique. Differences must be recognised and brought out and each one allowed to follow his own pursuits and interests, have his own friends and, above all, occupy his own special and exclusive place not only in your heart—which he will have anyway—but in your day. The last is often the most difficult to achieve because the more children you have, the more pieces you have to tear yourself into, to keep everyone happy. But children have an inborn sense of fairness, even if they may not always observe it, and they will quite readily accept that some time during the twenty-four hours each one has ten exclusive minutes with you. Special chats at bedtime, when each twin can enjoy a relaxed tête-à-tête with his mother or father, are great equalisers in many households, and if it is possible to take each child out separately from time to time, so much the better.

GOING TO SCHOOL

While the twins are small, your friendship with another mother will determine what company they keep. Once they go to nursery school or playgroup, each will make his own friends. A mother should understand that if her Johnny wants to invite your David around for tea, she does not have to invite his twin as well. Many mothers automatically feel they must always invite 'the twins'. This is neither necessary nor beneficial, as a twin may prefer to be alone with the other child or remain at home with you. For all that, one should not make a fetish of separateness; if they prefer to be together, in company or not, let them. Be guided by their own desires while they are little. Unless you are a believer in the 'stiff upper lip' syndrome and 'making a man of him', there is nothing to be gained from a forced and painful parting.

When the children start playgroup or nursery school, give each a name tag or other means of quick identification and have a word with the leader or teacher to ensure that she knows who is who and treats them quite separately. Squash anyone who refers to them in their hearing as 'the twins' or who compares them to each other in performance, ability, looks or anything else. Let them not be treated as two peas in a pod even if they look like it to some people.

At school, the question may arise as to whether they should be put into the same or different classes. No hard or fast rules should be applied, since so much depends on the individual children and their attitude to each other, as well as the school alternatives offered. For many children who start school at an early age, the enforced absence from home is difficult and even painful. For twins, whether they adore each other or not, the presence of the other is a great help in overcoming the forebodings that the strange new world of school can bring with it. To have such a friend and ally, with whom one can share this new experience and who can give one courage, is an enviable state of affairs and no one should take it away without good reason.

As they find their feet, different considerations may apply. They may be over-dependent on each other (this is more likely with identicals) or one may be dominant, constantly overshadowing the other who may or may not be content to hide in the other's shadow. In such cases, it may be better to put them in separate classes or even different schools at an age where this makes sense—for instance, when the transition occurs from infant to junior school.

In her study of identical twins, Dorothy Burlingham pointed out that the twin relationship differed from that of ordinary siblings in that the children have equal status, and neither can claim the prerogatives of the elder nor the indulgence usually accorded to the young. Their envies and jealousies, therefore, could not be settled by adopting either the stronger or the weaker role as siblings usually do. Mrs Burlingham found that the twins' growing need for each other acted as a powerful check to the negative feelings which arose from envy, jealousy and competition. These twin children could be observed to develop two emotional ties at the early stage when other children establish one tie only—to their mother. Twins have a double task: on the one hand, to solve the conflicts between love and hate separately in each relationship and, on the other hand, to find a balance between their love for their parents and their love for each other.

As they grow up, the very bond which unites twins can also complicate their lives. Schools which encourage a highly competitive element may not provide the ideal rearing ground. Involvement in group situations should give each a chance to develop his skills and social sense, and any opportunity for them to go in different directions should be investigated.

If both are musical, let each learn to play a different instrument. If both are artistic, let their talent be developed in different art forms. If both are budding linguists, encourage each to learn a different language where possible.

Parents in general, but particularly of twins, may feel it would be impossible to educate their children very differently from each other. But, on the assumption that parents try to provide the best education they can for each child, then what is right for one child is not necessarily right for another. The non-academic twin may achieve his potential more readily in a school geared to his preferences and ability in mechanical skills than in the one where his brother is being streamed for 'A' levels. It would be a mistake to treat them alike out of a misguided sense of fairness, or to think that it would be wrong to pay for the education of one and send the other to a state school.

When Natalie passed her 11-plus but Janice did not, the parents let Natalie go to grammar school but sent Janice to a private school so that she would not suffer from comparison of her ability. That would seem to be the right type of decision to make, as long as the private school provided a good scholastic alternative.

Fairness is to ensure that as far as possible each child has the same opportunities to develop his talents and skills in the way best suited to him—and not in paying an identical bill.

Twins who co-exist without any apparent need to follow in each other's footsteps, to outdo the other or to prove to the teacher that they are the tops, will probably develop quite happily in the same class. It is a good idea, however, to check with their teachers as to their individual progress, not only as one would for any single child, but to make sure that the other twin's presence in class is not a handicap. School sometimes reveals a completely different relationship from the one that prevails at home. A check should also be made to see that the teachers know each child and take the trouble to assess each one individually and not by comparison with his twin.

According to some teachers, parents sometimes give one twin undue responsibility with regard to the other. Whereas it is common place for an older child to be made responsible for a younger child, care should be exercised not to over-burden one twin in this respect; they are, after all, the same age.

DISCIPLINE

The problems of discipline can be quite different from those encountered with single children. Every family creates its own internal laws of what is permissible, what one might be able to get away with and what is definitely not allowed. How should these rules of conduct be enforced?

If both twins contravene the laws of the house, whatever form of discipline is chosen must obviously be applied to both culprits. But when only one has been naughty, the situation can be more complicated. Very often, one child cannot bear to see his twin being punished. So, when Marcus was chastised, it was Quentin who cried. When Dominic was told off, Annette put her hands over his ears. In another family, one toddler pulled her erring twin out of the room, away from a possible smack.

In one case, Quentin, the good twin, was so completely miserable at the prospect of his adored, naughty brother being told off that it became impossible to do more than remonstrate with the culprit in the gentlest—and totally ineffective—tones. Anything more drastic would have made Quentin suffer, whereas Marcus, who deserved the ticking off, would not have cared anyway. Since the parents did not want to punish the innocent, they had to wait until Quentin recognised that his twin was being anti-social; only then could any attempt be made to do something about it.

There are, of course, circumstances where safety considerations outweigh any moral scruples about upsetting the non-offender. Any child trying to gain first-hand experience of how the electric wiring works, or in any other way endangering himself or anyone else, must obviously be given to understand conclusively that this is not allowed under any circumstances, regardless of the other twin's sensitivity.

The bond which can complicate discipline is a positive advantage in terms of the comfort and consolation which many twins derive from each other. When Margie's mother asked her whether she had cried when the playgroup leader told her off for being naughty, she said, 'No. I just put my head on Anna's shoulder.' Another set of twins had an unspoken rule that if, at school, one was punished in error for the other, he just accepted it, without pointing out the mistake.

In all relationships, there is a dominant partner, one who calls the tune, one who is more aggressive than the other. Sometimes the weaker or more placid one suffers as a result. When they are too small to have any but the most basic emotions—such as, 'I don't like you at this moment. Therefore, I will clobber you'—it is better to separate real fighters as much as possible. Give them less opportunity to get on each other's nerves. Separate playpens may be the answer, and push chairs where the basher can sit in front of his passive victim rather than beside him. Once they reach an age of some sort of reason, children frequently fare best if left to sort out their own differences. They soon develop a code of morals which, if they are left to get on with it, will take care of their squabbles in an equitable way without parental intervention. Obviously if one child is constantly getting the worst of it, the mother must step in not only to stop any bullying but to prevent a relationship developing with entrenched positions.

Bribery may be corrupt, but it is terribly effective and usually a better method of getting what you want from your children than the threat or meting out of punishment. In the situation where one twin cannot bear to watch the other being chastised, it may be much easier for him to accept that he has earned a piece of chocolate or his choice of bedtime story whereas his naughty twin does not deserve the treat.

As with all forms of discipline, whatever else you fail to do, be consistent. Do not promise or threaten things which you cannot or will not do. All children can sense chinks in the parental armour, and twins have only to glance at each other fleetingly in order to launch a concerted attack on the finest hairline of a crack and then you are lost. Two imploring, pleading faces are very difficult to counter except with a stony heart—and this book is not written for people with stony hearts.

PLAY TIME

The marvellous thing about having twins, says everyone, is that they always have each other to play with. This is true most of the time, although some twins may not be able to amuse themselves amicably for any length of time and others may have periods of great friendship interspersed with episodes of mutual disdain. Some play situations can lead to fights, too. The desire for toys and playthings is the same for all children, but with twins there are two factors which have to be taken into consideration. The first concerns safety. Hammering toys, small but heavy model cars, sharp pencils and crayons, and swings can be particularly dangerous when two similarly minded and equally aged children want to use them at the same time. Although none is risky in itself, you must consider your children's temperaments and their ability to take turns or share before letting them play with such things. Twins are also great givers of Dutch courage to each other; what one would not contemplate doing on his own, two together will do with impunity.

One pair prepared a delightful surprise for their mother on Christmas morning. They 'cooked' breakfast, emptying every herb and spice into a pudding basin which then inadvertently got spilled on the floor; the house smelled like an oriental bazaar for weeks afterwards. Another mother recounts that her twins were playing particularly peacefully and quietly in their playroom one afternoon. Wanting to have a peep, she opened the door quietly only to discover that they were busy painting everything in sight with the lipstick found in the handbag she had left there. Sadder still is the tale of the gold bracelet removed from a mother's bedside table at 6 am and then 'taken up to the moon' by the twins tipper truck—and it never, ever returned!

PERSONAL POSSESSIONS

For the first year or two, the twins will probably have the same toys: two baby walkers, two sets of stacking beakers, two teddy bears, two tricycles. If you try to buy different kinds, they will no doubt both want the same one. As time elapses, this will change and the second consideration, to let each one have his own possessions, will become important. Twins of the opposite sex may quickly show individual preferences anyway and some toys, such as bricks or board-games, will obviously be bought for both jointly; but, increasingly, each new toy will be greeted with the words 'Is it just mine or do I have to share it?'

It matters very much to each child to have his own possessions. Even seemingly identical things have minute differences which twins are quick to spot, enabling one to say 'This one is mine.' Even where a game is intended to be played jointly, it is better to give it to one twin as belonging to him. As they get older, having separate possessions will encourage them to assume some degree of responsibility for looking after them. A special chest of drawers for each may indeed be the most valued present of all.

When they are old enough, it may help their development to let each one keep a different pet. One twin remembers that he opted for a kitten as soon as his brother asked for a puppy. Both had suffered from the constant sharing of everything—from a bar of chocolate to a toy—and although, on looking back, he is not sure they did not both want a cat, each was so anxious to have a possession of his own and unlike his brother's, that by unspoken agreement both chose different pets.

Whatever the difficulties of being a twin, the one element

lacking in their childhood is boredom. Many of the children I spoke to were aware of boredom whenever their twin was absent, but never when they were together. This applied even when the two did not get on. A partner for every game is, after all, paradise on earth if you are a child. But one little girl mentioned that they could not play hide and seek together successfully, as they were incapable of hiding from each other.

GROWING UP

If it has not happened already, there will almost certainly be a loosening of the twin bonds as they become adolescent and start forming emotional ties with members of the opposite sex. Occasionally twins marry twins, but sometimes they find each other's choice difficult to understand because it is so far removed from the common ground they once shared. Perhaps this reaction is a natural desire to be really free of the twin bond or perhaps it is the very opposite—a degree of hostility towards the first outsider to threaten the twin relationship.

What is it like being married to a twin? Some wives and husbands find it slightly disconcerting the first few times they are confronted with the double with whom they have no special relationship. But adult identical twins who live apart do grow less alike, at least superficially, and the other twin is usually recognised as a different person quite quickly, so that any initial embarrassment soon disappears.

It does not seem to be a common party trick for twins to pretend to be each other, but confusion does occur, sometimes not quite in the usual way. A surgeon, who had just finished a major operation on a middle-aged twin, saw what he took to be her ghost coming down the hospital corridor towards him and thought for a moment that she must have died.

Children, although often more perceptive than adults, can also be confused. Robert, the bearded father of three, has an identical twin brother, John, who is clean shaven. Late one night, Robert decided to shave off his beard. When, next morning, the three children burst into their parents' bedroom, one roared with laughter, one burst into tears and the third said, 'Why is Uncle John in bed with you, mummy?' They made their father promise to grow his beard again immediately!

The best story of all is David's. He went into a crowded restaurant to eat. The downstairs room was full, so he started going up the open staircase to the first floor. As he came to the halfway landing, he was amazed to see his identical twin coming up the other arm of the staircase. Exclaiming 'Fancy meeting you here!', he ran straight into a mirror, much to the astonishment of the diners below!

11 Twin Reflections

What do adult twins have to say about their childhood? What do they think their parents did wrong? What would they do differently if they had twins themselves?

All the twins to whom I spoke were unanimous in their rejection of identical clothes. Most disliked the comments and curiosity aroused in strangers. None wanted to be exploited as a party trick. Many went out of their way, once they grew up, to be as different as possible from each other. 'And which one are you?' was a question universally disliked by identicals. Fraternals, on the other hand, quite secure in their separate identity, quite enjoyed the slight confusion they occasionally created.

Most twins suffered if they had one present to share between them. All preferred to have separate possessions. Some felt that parents tried too hard to be fair and consequently ended up being unfair. When one twin lost a special pen, a new one was bought for each. When one took a dislike to a certain cereal, the mother stopped buying it because 'the twins don't like Brand X any more'. Several twins felt that the other was favoured by one or both parents. Some identicals regretted that the only photographs of their childhood showed them both together; furthermore, they could not always identify themselves correctly.

All enjoyed the close companionship afforded by a twin in childhood, but the majority were content to break away from each other as they grew older. Even when the bonds were no longer tight, many still felt the need to impart special news to their twin rather than to others.

Most thought that if they had twins themselves—and none of them did—it was important to bring out their individuality. 'Sometimes when I looked in the mirror when

I was small, I wondered who I was,' said one. All who were lumped together as children thought it made it more difficult initially to relate to the outside world. Those given every chance to develop separately felt this was as it should be.

But, in the final analysis, whether the twins had fought with one another or not, and even though none could judge whether it would have been better to be born alone, they thought there was something rather good about being a twin: 'I mean, you're never bored, are you?'

Bibliography

Bulmer, M. G. *Biology of Twinning in Man* (Oxford University Press)

Burlingham, Mrs Dorothy. *Twins: A Study of Three Pairs of Identical Twins* (Imago Publishing Company Limited)

Gedda, Luigi. *Twins in History and Science* (Chas C. Thomas)

Hastings, J. editor. *Encyclopaedia of Religion and Ethics* (T. & T. Clark)

Mittler, Peter. *The Study of Twins* (Penguin)

Scheinfeld, Aran. *Twins and Supertwins* (Chatto & Windus)

Index